A Decade of Collecting

A Decade of Collecting

**The Anglo American
Johannesburg Centenary Trust
1986-1996**

Johannesburg Art Gallery

Text written by: Jillian Carman, Julia Charlton, Nessa Leibhammer
Editing: Sandy Shoolman
Design: Lynda Ward
Typesetting: Lynda Ward
Reproduction: Disc Express
Printing: Creda Press
Photography: Wayne Oosthuizen, Bob Cnoops

© Johannesburg Art Gallery, 1997

ISBN 1-874836-31-0

Johannesburg Art Gallery
Postal address: Box 23561, Joubert Park, 2044
Street address: Klein Street, Joubert Park
Tel: (011) 725-3130/80
Fax: (011) 720-6000

This catalogue was published to accompany the exhibition **A Decade of Collecting: The Anglo American Johannesburg Centenary Trust 1986-1996** which opened at the Johannesburg Art Gallery on 25 March 1997.

This catalogue was made possible with funding from the Anglo American Johannesburg Centenary Trust.

Front cover illustrations:

Chuck Close (b 1940 USA)
Alex 1992
colour wood-block print, 72,5 x 59 cm

Sir William Quiller Orchardson RA (1832-1910 UK)
Portrait of Hilda Orchardson 1894
oil on canvas, 12,8 x 96,1 cm

Tsonga
Nwana / **child figure**
fabric, tin, thread, glass seed beads, buttons

Back cover illustration:

Howard Hodgkin (b 1932 UK)
Venice, evening 1995
Hand-painted etching and aquatint with carborundum, 160 x 196,5 cm

Frontispiece:

Northern Nguni
Vessel
wood, pokerwork, brass, 40 x 35 x 35 cm

Although every effort has been made to trace and acknowledge copyright holders of images in this book, we have not been successful in a few cases. If notified, the publishers will be pleased to rectify any omissions at the earliest opportunity. All works reproduced are in the collection of the Johannesburg Art Gallery.

Contents

Foreword   1
Gavin Relly

Preface   3
Rochelle Keene

Mining Patronage at the Johannesburg Art Gallery   5
Jillian Carman

The Anglo Trust and Traditional Southern African Art   11
Nessa Leibhammer

The Anglo Trust and the Development of the Historic Collections   41
Jillian Carman

The Anglo Trust and the Contemporary South African
and International Collections   61
Julia Charlton

References   73

Bibliography   74

Foreword

A Decade of Collecting is an exhibition which has been arranged to mark the tenth anniversary of the Anglo American Johannesburg Centenary Trust. It also marks the important transitional process which the Johannesburg Art Gallery has undertaken in its determination to play a lively and imaginative role in our developing society. A country's institutions reflect, protect and determine its values and certainly in times of significant socio-political change it is particularly important that cultural institutions should test the viability of long-standing attitudes.

The Johannesburg Art Gallery has indeed asked itself a number of questions and over the last ten years has moved to realign its collections to reflect its position in Southern Africa as well as to expand its domestic and continental art base. Of course this has not involved turning its back on its valuable international collections. Indeed, during this period, many gaps in these collections have been filled, but of course current currency values make foreign purchases more and more difficult.

When the Anglo Trust was established, the Gallery initially turned its attention to acquiring important collections of Southern African art, some of which were owned overseas, and these have formed a base for subsequent acquisitions, and for the development of a unique African collection. But it will achieve nothing if it is not constantly exhibited. The Gallery has been assiduous in making sure that display and interpretation of the highest standard is available to visitors and particularly schools.

It is fascinating to watch the unfolding impact of indigenous art through this channel. The Trust is proud of the contribution it has been able to make to the pursuit of the Gallery's long-term goals.

GAVIN RELLY
Chairperson, The Anglo American Johannesburg Centenary Trust

Preface

This publication celebrates the unique support of the Anglo American Johannesburg Centenary Trust for the Johannesburg Art Gallery over a period of ten years. March 1997 marks a decade since the first purchase made by the Trust for the Gallery. This purchase was a superb collection of Southern African headrests which had been housed at MuseuMAfricA since 1950 and was about to be sold to an overseas buyer. The Jaques Collection was purchased by the Trust and, thanks to its intervention, can still be enjoyed by the Gallery's visitors. The following text celebrates this and many other examples of invaluable acquisitions which the patronage of the Trust has made possible.

The Trust was established as part of a donation of R6 000 000 to the City of Johannesburg, commemorating the centenary of the city. The Anglo American Corporation of South Africa, to the great fortune of the Johannesburg Art Gallery, made the decision to invest in the cultural life of this city, and indeed the nation, by supporting the Gallery's application as one of the centenary beneficiaries. The first part of the Gallery's application was for funds to extend the Lutyens building. This would double the exhibition space of the Gallery and also provide an administration wing, offices for the curators who were accommodated in an exhibition hall, a workshop for the technical staff, a conservation studio, a library, education studio and coffee shop. The Johannesburg City Council had already approved plans and building operations were to commence in 1983. Budgetary constraints would, however, preclude the Gallery from installing a lift to the new exhibition area and the coffee shop, a fountain to the north of the exhibition area and temperature and humidity controls to ensure that the whole Gallery would comply with international museum standards for the conditions under which works of art were displayed.

The Gallery also proposed the establishment of a trust fund. This would enable it to purchase internationally so as to keep abreast of contemporary trends and to develop the sound nucleus of its existing collection. While the Gallery's municipal grant provided funding for South African art purchases, the Gallery was finding it increasingly difficult to buy in other areas, given the significant increase in prices of international art compounded by import surcharges.

To our delight the Anglo American Corporation, through the offices of the then Chairperson, Mr Gavin Relly, accepted both proposals submitted by the Gallery and two dreams were realised. Of the donation of R6 000 000, R1 700 000 was spent on the building project, approximately R300 000 on the commissioning of four major sculptures for Joubert Park, and R4 000 000 invested in a trust fund, the interest of which is spent on purchases for the Gallery.

The Johannesburg Centenary Sculpture Competition, held in 1986 and funded by the Anglo American Corporation, enabled the Gallery to commission four sculptures. These are **Citizen** by Bruce Arnott, **Tightroping** by David James Brown, **Otjittinduua 11** by Willem Strydom and **Talion** by Gavin Younge, which stand proudly at the entrance to the Gallery, in the central sculpture garden, and in Joubert Park, for the enjoyment of all the citizens of our country and visitors to it.

The installation of air-conditioning and temperature controls in the Lutyens building has meant that the Gallery's old and new areas fully comply with international museum standards, and the refurbishment of the Lutyens building in bold fabric gave the grand old building the facelift it required.

The establishment of the Anglo American Johannesburg Centenary Trust has had major ramifications for the Gallery in terms of its acquisitions policy. In the first instance, it has enabled the Gallery to once again consider major purchases of contemporary international art and to augment its marvellous collections of 17th-century Dutch and early 20th-century British art. Details of purchases in these areas are highlighted in the contributions by the relevant curators of collections. In the second instance, it has enabled the Gallery to establish a collection of traditional Southern African art, a major gap in our collection until 1987 with the purchase of the Jaques Collection of headrests. The Gallery has, since that date, acquired collections of great importance both locally and abroad. These include the Horstmann Collection (1992) and the Brodie Collection (1995). The purchase of these and other artworks fulfils three important functions of this Gallery - to repatriate traditional objects to their country of origin for the benefit of all the people of this country, to promote a sense of pride in the cultural richness of this region and to become a major international centre for the study of Southern African art.

The lodging of Mr Harry Oppenheimer's Brenthurst Collection of traditional Southern African art at this Gallery in 1986 enabled us to establish the nucleus of aesthetically magnificent objects in the Johannesburg Art Gallery. In acknowledgement of the role played by Mr Harry Oppenheimer in Johannesburg, and especially his support of the Gallery and the cultural life of this city, the Anglo American Corporation presented a bust of Mr Oppenheimer by Rhona Stern to the Gallery in 1988. The bust was unveiled at a ceremony presided over by the then Chairperson of the Management Committee of the Johannesburg City Council, Alderman JF Oberholzer, JP.

The purchases made through the Trust have immeasurably enhanced the Gallery both nationally and internationally. I would like to record my thanks to the present curatorial staff of the Gallery whose expertise ensures that the collection is of world-class status: the Senior Curator of Collections, Thembinkosi Mabaso; the Curator of Historic Collections, Jillian Carman; the Curator of the traditional Southern African collection, Nessa Leibhammer and the Curator of Contemporary Collections, Julia Charlton.

In paying tribute to the Anglo American Johannesburg Centenary Trust, I should like to extend particular thanks to the former Chairperson, Sir Albert Robinson (1986 - 1993) and the present Chairperson, Mr Gavin Relly (1993 - present), as well as the trustees for their support. Decisions of the Art Gallery Committee, which in the first instance approves all acquisitions to the Gallery, whether by purchase, donation or bequest, are unfailingly endorsed by the trustees. The collection of the Gallery is being developed appropriately. Experts in the field of art are given the freedom to make decisions, while experts in the field of patronage are ensuring that the capital base of the fund is being enhanced. The Gallery can only flourish in such an environment.

ROCHELLE KEENE
Director, Johannesburg Art Gallery

Mining Patronage at the Johannesburg Art Gallery

When the Anglo American Corporation of South Africa Limited adopted the Johannesburg Art Gallery as a Johannesburg centenary project in 1986, it revived a tradition that had been dormant for seventy odd years. It re-established the supremacy of mining patronage at the Gallery.

Johannesburg owes its existence to mines. So too does its municipal art museum. The Johannesburg Art Gallery was founded in 1910 with mining money. Its first patrons were Florence Phillips and her husband Lionel, a director of the Central Mining and Investment Corporation and a past president of the Chamber of Mines. Other major donors were Otto Beit, administrator of the Beit Trust which derived its capital from mining interests, Max Michaelis, a retired director of Wernher, Beit & Co. and the mining magnates Sigismund Neumann, Abe Bailey, Friedrich Eckstein, Solly Joel and Julius Wernher.

After this generous start, there was little interest from the mining establishment until the Anglo American Johannesburg Centenary Trust was established in 1986. A comparison of these two episodes reveals not only the nature of mining patronage but also the nature of museums in South Africa at the beginning and end of the twentieth century.

The only other major donations in the Gallery's history – major denoting a gift significant enough to affect the nature of an existing collection – are the Howard Pim bequest of over 500 original prints in 1934 and the Eduard Houthakker gift of 16 Dutch paintings in 1947. These two gifts established a Print Cabinet and a collection of seventeenth-century Dutch paintings respectively, both coming from the patrons' private collections. Mining patrons' gifts, by contrast, were not originally their private possessions. The mining patrons in the 1910s provided money for an agent, director or curator to purchase artworks, they did not part with long-held possessions. The principal similarity between the two major mining gifts is this personal detachment from the gifts themselves.

At the Gallery's foundation, there was an acquisitions policy which was developed by the purchasing agent, Sir Hugh Lane, who does not seem to have been answerable to the donors or the Johannesburg Art Gallery in any significant way. Lane was the London-based curator of the Gallery-in-the-making, who began collating a nucleus of pictures and sculptures in 1909. He was in effect agent and curator combined. Checks were provided by the Art Gallery Committee in the early years, but these were after the collection had been created. The foundation – the nature – of the Gallery had already been established by the time the Gallery opened to the public in November 1910. The Johannesburg-based curator, Albert Gyngell, seems to have had little say in what was bought, deferring to decisions made by the London-based curators, Lane and his successor, Robert Ross. Accountability to the donors, as distinct from the Art Gallery Committee, seems to have been by way of private letter rather than committee.

In the implementation of the Anglo American Johannesburg Centenary Trust, acquisitions are recommended by the Gallery's director and curators following an acquisitions policy which they have formulated and which has been approved by members of the Art Gallery Committee and the former Johannesburg City Council. All new acquisitions are approved in the first instance by the Art Gallery Committee before being presented to the Trust's trustees, who include a Greater Johannesburg Transitional Metropolitan Council (GJTMC) representative. Donations are then reported to various GJTMC committees before they are formally accepted into the Gallery's collection. Despite these committee procedures, the Gallery has a large amount of autonomy, a hallmark of the Trust being that its administrators are not prescriptive, although they do require accountability.

The present-day curators have the function that Lane had in 1909 and 1910. In both instances the donors are characterised by their non-interference.

This degree of autonomy is desirable in present-day museum practice. It was admirable at the time the Gallery was founded although the lack of intervention eighty-five years ago suggests that the true interests of the donors lay elsewhere, and that social responsibility was dispensed without deep personal involvement. For example, the principal monetary donor, Otto Beit, is commemorated in the Gallery's collection by a William Orpen portrait of telling significance. Beit is shown seated in his London study surrounded by items from his personal collection: a Murillo series of the Prodigal Son and a collection of Renaissance bronzes. Not only are these totally different in nature from his donations to the Johannesburg Art Gallery, they were evidently never considered as possible donations to a South African art museum. Beit, like other mining magnates, chose to fulfil his obligation of returning wealth to the land from which it came through money rather than personal possessions. His collection is today in the Beit family's preferred motherland, Ireland, at the family home, Russborough, and the National Gallery of Ireland, Dublin.

Although the Johannesburg Art Gallery did not benefit from major private collections because its early donors were personally aloof from this new museum, it certainly gained on another front. The lack of personal intervention from donors – and, indeed, from the institution itself – resulted in an innovative acquisition policy which was the envy of progressive British art critics and curators in the 1910s.

Lane was evidently unique on the British art scene at that time in his ability to operate independently of the conservative art establishment. His freedom from the committee context, his eye for a good picture, and his financial resources combined to create exceptional collections and individual acquisitions. Recipients of his expertise and gifts included the Hugh Lane Municipal Gallery of Modern Art in Dublin (1908), the Johannesburg Art Gallery (1910) and the Michaelis Collection in Cape Town (1913), all of whose foundation collections were collated by Lane; the National Gallery of Ireland, of which he was director from 1914 until his death in 1915; the Frick Collection in New York; numerous private American collections ('he was one of the first to discover the great new race of American millionaires', O'Connor, 1915), and the National Gallery in London.

Over seventy years later, when the Anglo American Johannesburg Centenary Trust was established, the absence of donor intervention was one of its major strengths. In terms of the Trust, the purpose of the endowment is not to dictate what should be acquired but to enable the beneficiary to make acquisitions. The powers of the trustees reside in the administering and investment of the Trust, not in the decisions of how the Trust is to be used. Those decisions reside with the Johannesburg Art Gallery and the Art Gallery Committee.

Lane's autocratic working method would be unacceptable in today's public museum context, where consultation, representation and accountability are the desired operating norms. But it was an inspired way at that time of breaking the trustee stranglehold that was typical in British art museums, and which effectively excluded contemporary artists from their local museums at a time their works were being acquired for Dublin and

Johannesburg. Lavish praise for Lane's Johannesburg collection was expressed in the British press when it was displayed in London prior to the Johannesburg opening in November 1910. Lane's remarkable acquisitions, according to the critics, were possible because he was unfettered by the control of any committee or board of trustees. The collection was equally well received by the Johannesburg press, its innovative character being associated with the dynamism of a young town.

What was this collection for which such heady claims were made? It comprised about 129 items divided into European Schools of Painting (the major part of the collection), Portraits (intended as the nucleus of a National Portrait Gallery), Statuary, Etchings, Watercolours and Drawings, 'some interesting' donations that Lane considered more suitable for what he called the 'Museum Section' (of applied art) than the Modern Art Section, and some Medici reproductions (Johannesburg, 1910). In addition there were some uncatalogued applied art and craft items which Florence Phillips intended to be the basis of a School of Design and Museum of Industrial Art, but these projects were never realised. There was no representation of a South African school of painting. The only South African artist in the foundation collection was Anton van Wouw, who had five bronzes in the Statuary section.

It was an appropriate and fine collection for the 1910s and is still today a very useful education resource, while maintaining its international appeal. However, it had its limitations and these soon became apparent after its opening. The principal flaw is that Lane identified the best of modern art of his day with what was being produced in Britain, and the inclusion of other schools was merely in order to show the roots from which contemporary British art drew. These he identified as nineteenth-century French, Dutch and British Impressionists. Lane's approach excluded contemporary art-making on the European continent. There were no French Post-Impressionist, Fauve, Cubist or German Expressionist paintings. It also excluded art-making in South Africa as an identifiable school.

Lane's collection was an imported one which did not reflect the context into which it had been placed. It was inevitable, after the initial euphoria, that gaps in the collection would begin to be noticed, and that it would begin to adapt to its environment.

The inclusion of local South African artists was the first area of change, and by the 1980s this was the area which had developed the most. The filling of gaps in the foundation collection is another growth area, with the missing items or schools identified by Lane and subsequent curators. The most notable gap-fillers in relation to Lane's nucleus are in the field of Dutch Impressionism and British Modernism of the early twentieth century. Lane's 'good collection of Old Masters' that he hoped some public-spirited owner would 'some day be induced to lend, give or bequeath' (Johannesburg, 1910: i-ii) materialised with the Houthakker gift of seventeenth-century Dutch paintings in 1947. The need to live up to the foundation title of 'Municipal Gallery of Modern Art' has ensured that there has been a steady acquisition over the years of contemporary artworks, predominantly by South African artists with some international examples. There has also been a focused effort to represent the major movements in the history of twentieth-century art.

Until the mid 1980s the essential nature of the Johannesburg Art Gallery remained unchanged. It was a museum of western-tradition art. Although the South African collection eventually predominated, the examples collected and displayed continued in a western paradigm. 'Other' artmaking in Southern Africa was not collected. It was at this time that a combination of events effected the most significant developments in the Gallery's history, enabling it to break from its western mould and enter the Southern African art debate in a meaningful way. The 1980s was the watershed decade for the Johannesburg Art Gallery.

The first event of significance was the approval of extensions to the Gallery's Edwin Lutyens building. Lutyens' plans were only partially completed when the building opened in Joubert Park in 1915. Two side pavilions were added 1938-40, but the original Lutyens plan was still incomplete and the collection continued to be inadequately housed. The 1980s finally saw the provision of the space originally planned for the Gallery. Meyer Pienaar and Partners Inc were appointed the architects for the extensions, which were officially opened on 22 October 1986.

The second significant event was the appointment as director in November 1983 of Christopher Till, the former director of the National Gallery of Zimbabwe in Harare. He brought experience of networking with museums in Africa and with the UNESCO-affiliated International Council of Museums, both contacts denied to South African institutions at that time. He also brought experience of transforming a colonial art gallery into an institution more appropriate to its African context. The radical changes in acquisition and exhibition policies at the Gallery in the 1980s occurred under the directorship of Till, who stated publicly on his appointment as director that he intended to build up a collection of traditional Southern African art.

The third event of significance in the watershed 1980s was the securing of the most important patronage since the Gallery's inception, the Anglo American Johannesburg Centenary Trust. The Johannesburg Art Gallery's annual report (1984/1985) notes that

> This donation marks a new era in the Gallery's activities and is one of the most important events in the history of the Gallery. It will enable the Gallery to preserve its collection in the best possible way and to build significantly onto the collection first put together in 1909 by Lady Phillips with the assistance and advice of Sir Hugh Lane. (. . .) The first donations to the Gallery came from the early Rand Lords and mining magnates in the first decade of this century. The wheel has turned full circle with this donation by the Anglo American Corporation.

The R4 000 000 endowment came into being as The Anglo American Johannesburg Centenary Trust on 22 April 1986, one of the most important gifts to a South African art museum in recent history.

The Deed of Trust of the Anglo American Johannesburg Centenary Trust (22 April 1986) outlines the purposes and the powers of the trustees, making it clear that the independence of the Gallery's acquisition policy is honoured. It was agreed at the Trust's inception that the money should be used to enhance the existing collection by purchasing works internationally and locally which normally would not be affordable with a modest institutional budget. Particular areas identified were contemporary international, expatriate South African, examples that show the development of modern art, and generally building on the existing strengths of the collection. But perhaps the most significant area was the realignment of the Gallery's acquisition policy with the establishment of a traditional African collection. The first acquisition with money generated by the Trust acts as a statement of policy in this regard. The Jaques Collection of headrests was bought in March 1987, the first items of traditional Southern African art to enter the collection.

Three characteristics of how the Trust would develop over the next ten years are apparent in this first acquisition. Firstly, it enables the Gallery to make major purchases. Secondly, the Trust empowers the Gallery to alter the direction of acquisitions and the inherited nature of the collection. And thirdly, the Trust aids the retention in this country, or the repatriation, of cultural objects in the quest for reclaiming the previously-neglected histories and cultures of the majority of South Africans. These characteristics apply principally to the area of traditional Southern African art, in which field most of the acquisitions over the past ten years have been made. The change in the acquisition and display policy is radical and visible.

One of the aims expressed in the Deed of Trust (22 April 1986) is to finance the acquisition of works of art 'whilst recognising the terms and conditions under which the Art Gallery was established and its initial collection donated (...)'. This refers to the modern and international nature of the foundation collection. The Trust has not been used only to forge radical new directions. It has also been used to enhance the existing collection, to make it more coherent visually and historically, and thereby to make it a more effective educational tool. Acquisitions here have been made in two principal areas: strengthening the existing historic European collection, and widening the contemporary international and South African collection.

Most of the historic acquisitions are in keeping with Sir Hugh Lane's original concept. They enhance his 'British Moderns' and nineteenth-century Dutch Impressionist collections, and build on the foundations he laid – the subsequently-founded seventeenth-century Dutch collection, which he hoped someone would donate, and modern art post 1910.

The contemporary international collection has been enhanced principally by works on paper, reflecting a policy decision to purchase in this medium. The Gallery already had a strong representation of contemporary print-making, and purchasing in this field has enabled the Gallery to obtain a wide and representative range. In the contemporary South African area, some of the most significant acquisitions have emanated from two sculpture competitions funded by the Anglo American Corporation, the first launched in May 1985 (outside the parameters of the Trust) and the second in June 1990. Sculptures by Bruce Arnott, David James Brown, Willem Strydom, Gavin Younge, Andries Botha and Peter Schütz entered the collection in this way.

Overlaps occur between the three principal collecting areas of traditional Southern African, historic and contemporary international and South African art, just as they occur between the different curatorial disciplines. These dynamic, significant purchases interact across boundaries with each other and with the existing Johannesburg Art Gallery collection, which they were purchased to enhance.

The Johannesburg Art Gallery has transformed, through its collections, facilities and activities, into an institution that the original patrons would barely recognise. There is talk about mining patronage at the Gallery coming full circle. How ironic that the new boy on the block, Ernest Oppenheimer, should have been snubbed by Sir Lionel Phillips 'sitting in slightly decadent glory in the tradition of the Randlords who had most of them now faded from the scene' (Hocking 1973:74) when he tried to sell Phillips the Consolidated Mines Selection Company's various interests in 1916. In time, Oppenheimer's Anglo American Corporation, established in September 1917, not only owned all Phillips' mining interests, but also enabled the art museum Phillips helped found to develop radically beyond its foundation collection.

JILLIAN CARMAN
Curator: Historic Collections

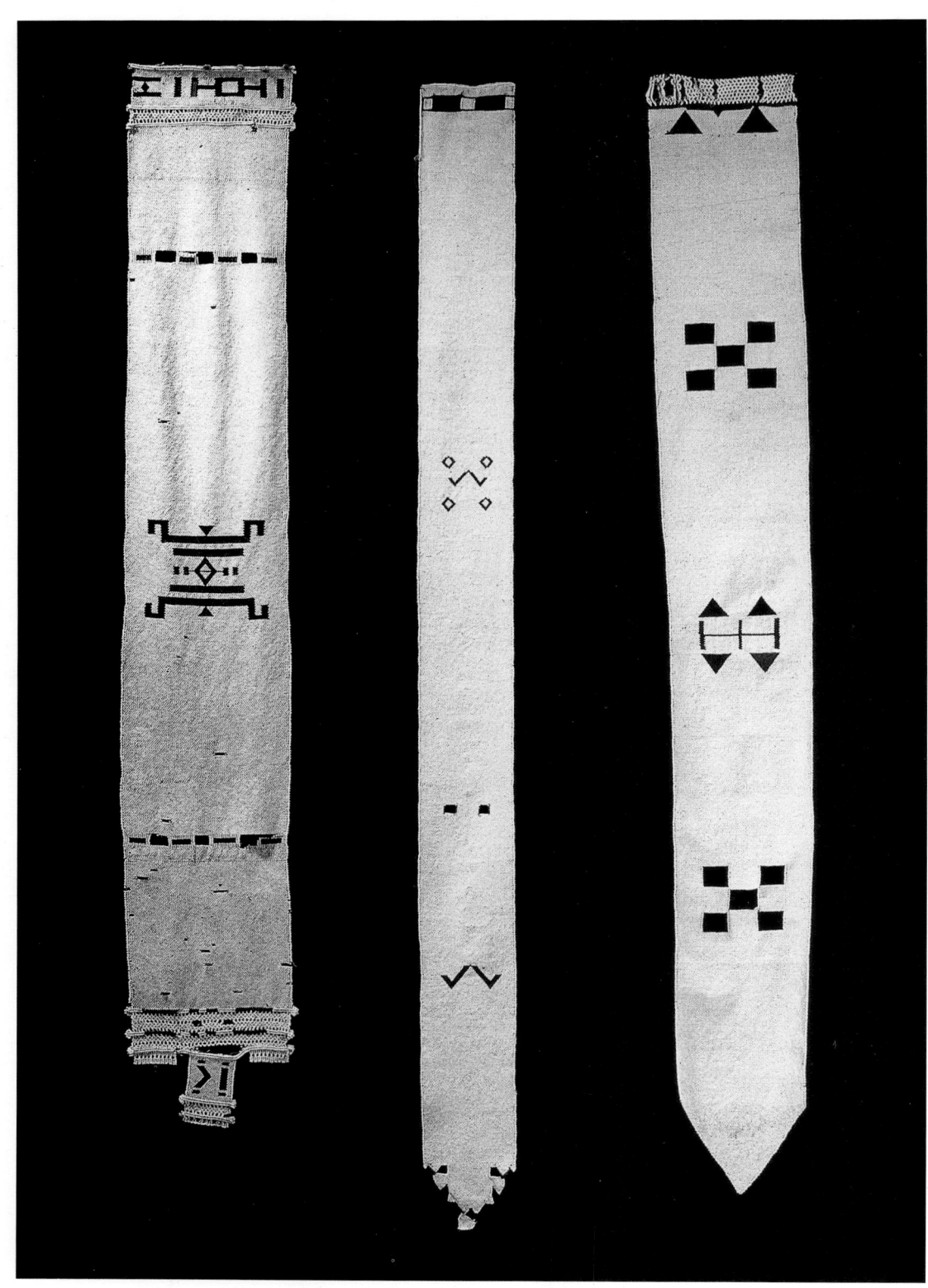

▲ Ndebele
Inyoka / beaded panels

The Anglo Trust and Traditional Southern African Art

For many centuries black African cultures produced a diverse, complex and unique range of objects which remained largely unknown or poorly comprehended in the western world. A few of these works were admired for their formal beauty but most were seen as war trophies, ethnographic specimens, curios or evidence of heathen practices. This attitude has undergone a radical shift and in the last twenty years art galleries in Southern Africa have begun to collect and display traditional works. The Anglo American Johannesburg Centenary Trust has enabled the Johannesburg Art Gallery to build up one of the finest collections of traditional art in the region.

Consistent undervaluing of the cultural heritage by collectors, scholars and museums in South Africa resulted in many of the finest pieces leaving in the hands of missionaries, traders and travellers and many are now to be found in museum basements and private collections in Europe and America. Those that remained were placed in natural history or ethnographic museums.

Since the 1970s, traditional Southern African works have been recognised as belonging to an international cultural and aesthetic heritage. Art historians have also started to see them as valuable evidence in the reconstruction of histories distorted by previous political dispensations. Objects can show us how people saw themselves, what their cultural practices were and how they interacted with other cultures. For example, beadwork is a marker of identity. Evidence gleaned from beadwork patterns and colours dated to the late 19th and early 20th century reveals complex relationships between people and contradicts the apartheid notion of a country populated by discrete 'ethnic' identities.

In the 1970s collectors and dealers began to realise the potential monetary value of work from South Africa and exported objects to be sold on international markets. Because these works had not been considered valuable or significant, few laws existed to prevent their export. It was therefore imperative that art galleries in South Africa responded to this situation. Concern arose to secure works which were in danger of being exported and also to repatriate works which had left the country.

The Johannesburg Art Gallery made its first purchase of traditional Southern African art in 1987 with funds provided by the Anglo American Johannesburg Centenary Trust. The Gallery purchased 114 headrests collected by the Reverend A P Jaques in the Pilgrim's Rest area of Mpumalanga. Collected in the 1920s and 1930s these wooden pillows are of Tsonga, Shona, Swazi and Zulu origin. The Jaques family had lent this collection to MuseuMAfricA but then decided, with a few exceptions, to sell it. Few South African institutions were able to raise the necessary funds. The Gallery was fortunate to acquire the collection and prevent its further dispersion or export.

Works made before 1900 are almost always purchased from overseas. The Gallery has, so far, acquired three such collections. In 1989 the Gallery purchased a small group of objects assembled from Britain, North America and Europe by the Swiss collector Udo Horstmann. These include body ornaments from the Ovahimba people of north-west Namibia, carved wooden spoons from Swaziland and a figure from Tanzania.

This was followed in 1992 by a particularly fine selection of 26 objects from the same collector.

These include a Tswana knife carved in bone, rare carved figures from the Northern Province and a selection of staffs, one of which is said to have been removed from Cetshwayo's kraal after the Battle of Ulundi. A Tsonga headrest with an elephant motif and an unusual Nguni seat, both of exceptional quality and rarity, also form part of this collection. Many of these objects are no longer made in Southern Africa.

The third overseas purchase, made in 1995, consists of a small but rare collection of beaded items from Michael Graham-Stewart, a London-based dealer. These are mostly provenanced to the 19th century and are of an age and quality seldom seen. These factors, together with the high prices fetched by works on international markets which is exacerbated by the unfavourable rand exchange rate, would make it impossible for the Gallery to repatriate works from overseas without funding from the Anglo American Johannesburg Centenary Trust.

Also in 1995, the Gallery purchased a large collection of traditional objects, mostly beaded items made between 1930 and 1970. This collection was assembled by Mordechai Brodie, a dealer working for over a decade in the field in Southern Africa, who meticulously recorded information relating to the objects collected. Since most traditional works come with little or no documentation, this added to the already significant value of the collection. The Gallery staff selected 467 of the finest pieces to add to its holdings.

Many of the traditional Southern African items purchased by the Gallery with trust funds are now displayed in two installations **Secular and Spiritual: Objects of Mediation** and **Views from Within**.

The Johannesburg Art Gallery aims to make its traditional Southern African collection fully representative of the cultural heritage of black South Africans. Placing these works in an art gallery celebrates their cultural and spiritual significance and recognises them as art, restoring dignity to the cultures which created them.

NESSA LEIBHAMMER
Curator: Traditional Southern African Collection

▶ Zulu
Iziqhaza / earplugs

▼ Zulu
Iziqhaza / earplugs

▲ Zulu
Imbenge / beer pot cover

▼ Zulu
Imbenge / beer pot cover

▲ Zulu
Imbenge / beer pot cover

▼ Zulu
Imbenge / beer pot cover

Iziqhaza / earplugs
wood, plastic, paint, steel pins
5.3 to 7.3 x 0.8 to 1 cm
acquired 1995 from Mordechai Brodie, Johannesburg

Amongst Zulu people ear-piercing is essential for 'opening the inner hearing' (Brodie 1986: interview). A person with pierced ears is thought to be able to hear the ancestors. The stigma attached to a person who has not had this done is similar to the one affecting the uncircumcised amongst groups such as the Mfengu. These people are considered childlike and incompetent however old they may be.

While many people had pierced ears, very stretched earlobes were seen predominantly on men and women from the Msinga area of KwaZulu-Natal. These people would wear a plug of wood up to 7 cm in diameter. Although these large earplugs or *iziqhaza* were found in some other areas of KwaZulu-Natal, the wearer usually came from or had strong family connections to the Msinga area.

Plugs made in the late 19th and early 20th century were often simple round, smooth, solid wooden forms. Cylindrical snuff-boxes made from reed, bone, horn or wood were also worn through the ear. Later pieces were carved through with patterns like fretwork which made them lighter. From about the 1940s with the development of commercial plastics, intricately inlaid plastic attached with pins to a wooden disk became popular. Sometimes 40 or 50 pieces of plastic were used in a single pair of plugs. During the late 1950s and 1960s designs were painted on wood with enamel paint. The 1970s saw brass and chrome studs being used. Modern pieces in Msinga and Johannesburg, made by men from the Msinga area, use perspex and other modern materials.

The tradition of having excessively stretched earlobes is dying out. One of the reasons may be that the past political dispensation made it dangerous to be easily identifiable as belonging to a particular area or group. People have been known to surgically restore their earlobes to their original shape. Today *iziqhaza* are constructed from two disks of wood covered with plastic which are secured together in the centre with elastic and are simply clipped onto the earlobe when needed.

Izimbenge / baskets
plant fibre, telephone wire, glass seed beads
14.6 to 23.0 x 3 to 8 cm
acquired 1995 from Mordechai Brodie, Johannesburg

Izimbenge are small grass baskets about 15 to 25 centimetres in diameter. Zulu men originally wove these fine baskets while women added the beadwork decorations. Beadwork designs and colours are linked to the identity of the maker and user. The bowl or saucer-like shape often has a small indented centre on which the *imbenge* can stand when turned upside down. Undecorated *izimbenge* can be used for serving food, while the more elaborately embellished ones cover the *ukhamba* or beer vessel when it is full of beer.

The introduction of materials such as copper and plastic-covered telephone wire have allowed new designs and techniques to develop. At first the techniques used imitated grass weaving but later other techniques, made possible by the use of wire, were developed. By the end of the 1980s individual artists, including a number of women, were producing only for the commercial markets. Many are recognisable by their particular styles and designs.

Isiphephetu, Jogolo and Liphoto / women's aprons

Isiphephetu / maiden's apron
canvas, thread, glass seed beads
46 x 35.5 cm
acquired 1995 from Mordechai Brodie, Johannesburg

Isiphephetu / maiden's apron
canvas, thread, glass seed beads
32 x 43 cm
acquired 1995 from Mordechai Brodie, Johannesburg

Jogolo / married woman's ceremonial apron
hide, thread, glass seed beads
55.5 x 55 cm
acquired 1995 from Mordechai Brodie, Johannesburg

Jogolo / married woman's ceremonial apron
canvas, glass seed beads, metal beads
67 x 56 cm
acquired 1995 from Mordechai Brodie, Johannesburg

Liphoto / married woman's apron
canvas, thread, glass seed beads
55 x 52.5 cm
acquired 1995 from Mordechai Brodie, Johannesburg

Liphoto / married woman's apron
canvas, thread, glass seed beads
51 x 52 cm
acquired 1995 from Mordechai Brodie, Johannesburg

Beaded aprons or skirts indicate the social status of the women who wear them. In most cases, they indicate whether a young woman is pre- or post-initiation, available for courting or engaged, newly married or a mother. They also show the social standing of the woman, whether she is a first or second wife or the wife of an important person.

Around puberty a young girl undergoes some form of initiation to mark her transition into womanhood or child-bearing status. The initiation usually takes place over a period of months, although with the pressures of urban living this is sometimes shortened.

Completion of maidens' initiation is marked by the wearing of a particular apron. A young Ndebele girl replaces her short fringed apron (*gabi*) with a stiff rectangular panel (*isiphephetu*) which is made by her mother. The beads are stitched onto a canvas back which is stretched over a piece of board. Although these were traditionally worn every day, the contemporary *isiphephetu* is unwieldy and only worn on ceremonial occasions.

After marriage, women again wear specific aprons. The Ndebele ceremonial apron is called the *jogolo* while the *liphoto* is the apron used everyday. The *jogolo* is a wide panel of leather or canvas which is extensively if not fully beaded. It has five main flaps and sometimes two smaller ones at the sides. The significance of these flaps remains unclear. The *liphoto* resembles the *jogolo* in size but instead of the five flaps it has two square flaps at either end with a row of fringes between. It is said that the two square flaps represent the husband and wife and the fringes represent the children.

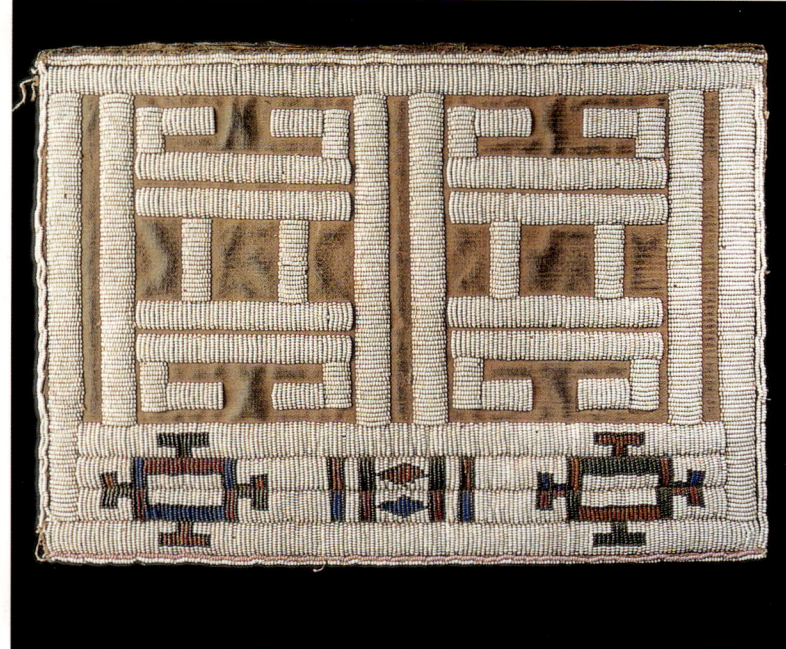
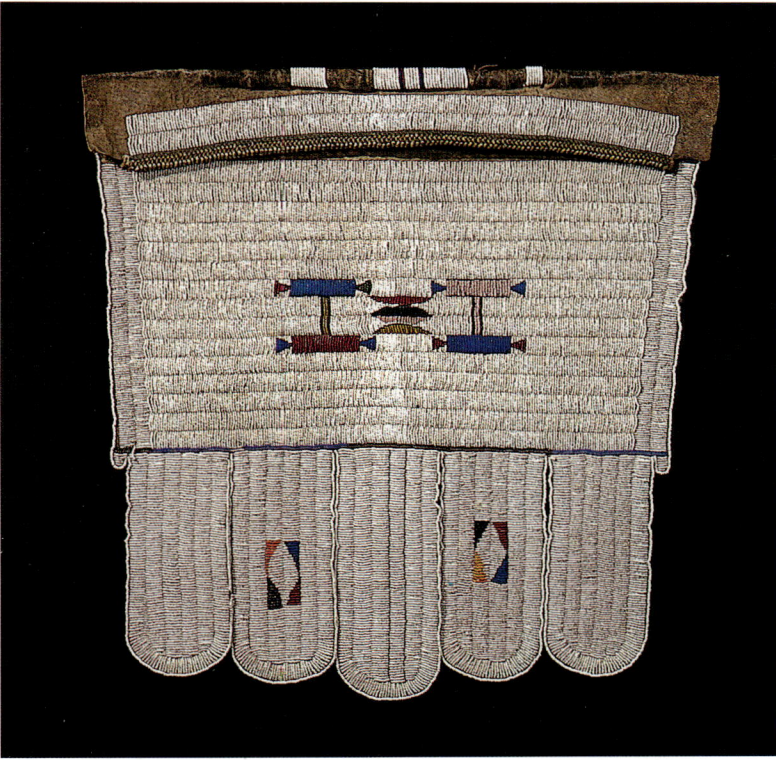
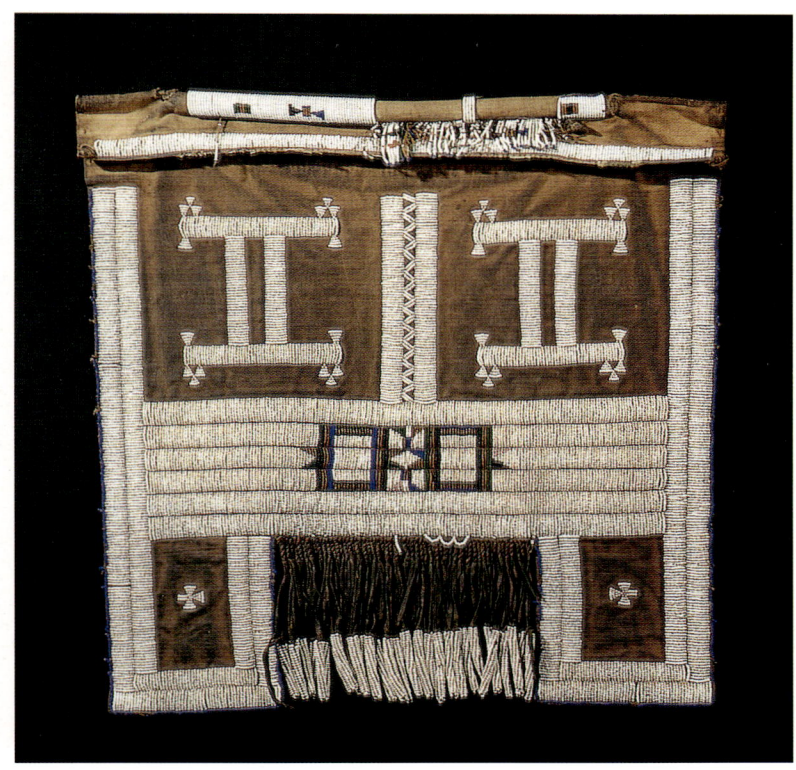

◄ Ndebele
Liphoto / married woman's apron

▲ Ndebele
▲ *Isiphephetu* / maiden's apron

▲ Ndebele
Jogolo / married woman's ceremonial apron

▲ Ndebele
▲ *Isiphephetu* / maiden's apron

▲ Ndebele
Liphoto / married woman's apron

Inyoka / beaded panels

Inyoka / beaded panel
thread, glass seed beads, wool, buttons
145 × 23,5 cm
acquired 1995 from Mordechai Brodie, Johannesburg

Inyoka / beaded panel
thread, glass seed beads
152 × 20,5 cm
acquired 1995 from Mordechai Brodie, Johannesburg

Inyoka / beaded panel
thread, glass seed beads
156 × 13 cm
acquired 1995 from Mordechai Brodie, Johannesburg

The *nyoka*, meaning snake, is a long panel of beads worn hanging down the back of an Ndebele bride at her wedding. Because it is constructed entirely of thread and beads without any backing it is very flexible. Many of the earlier *inyoka* are almost entirely white, a colour associated with periods of transition. The *nyoka* is thought to signify the changing status of the woman, a phallic element and the presence of the ancestors.

Most *inyoka* have a strap or band from which they are hung on the body. Other *inyoka* are sewn onto the *linaga*, a skin cape made by a bride's father. These are kept by the woman and embellished with further beadwork throughout her life.

Irari / blanket
fabric, thread, glass seed beads
140 × 110 cm
acquired 1995 from Mordechai Brodie, Johannesburg

One of the items of Ndebele clothing which is still very much in use is the blanket or *irari*. Blankets sold in South Africa were originally produced in Europe. The first type of blanket available to Ndebele people in what was then the Transvaal was a red blanket with patterns. But Ndebele people have always been involved in developing and changing fashions, so other blankets and patterns were later adopted. The most popular of these is the 'Middelburg' blanket with its green, red, blue, yellow and brown stripes.

Women decorate their blankets as they wish. The most common form of decoration is long strips of beadwork which are either worked onto the edges of the blanket or sewn on after completion, but many have little or no beadwork at all.

Mporiana / chest piece
mixed media
54 × 29 cm
acquired 1995 from Mordechai Brodie, Johannesburg

This elaborately decorated item is worn as a chest ornament.

Mthambothi / *thambothi* necklaces
wood, glass beads, mixed media
47 to 67 cm
acquired 1995 from Mordechai Brodie, Johannesburg

Talisman necklaces are worn mostly by older Ndebele men and women. The individual wooden pieces are carefully carved, often in the shape of diviner's tablets (*hakata*) and sometimes with more local, specific meaning. The carvers are always older men and the pieces are believed to assist in the bringing of good fortune or at least preventing bad luck.

Most of the women who wear them associate *thambothi* pieces with ancestors but in a vague way, saying it makes the ancestors happy (Brodie, 1985: interview with Ndebele women). Most of the men, some of them carvers, have more to say about the origin and power of these necklaces. Firstly, they seem to have been carved after a significant episode or crisis in a person's life – the loss of a loved one, a misfortune like cattle loss or drought, or a powerful dream or image. This is followed by a visit to a healer and sacrifice to the ancestors. During this crisis or following it, the *thambothi* is carved as a therapeutic means of embodying the experience.

In addition to the carved pieces of wood, a *thambothi* necklace has glass beads, usually old and therefore associated with previous generations, or dung beads (made of a combination of cow dung and sawdust or grass and sand) which are also associated with the ancestors but through cattle. Special beads made from pieces of metal or ornaments are also incorporated to raise the consciousness and increase the personal power of the wearer. The wood of the *thambothi* exudes a pleasant smell and is used for medicinal purposes, but is slightly toxic making it unsuitable for the carving of eating utensils.

Khozo / brass beads
brass
18 to 62 x 0,8 to 45 cm
acquired 1995 from Mordechai Brodie, Johannesburg

Small, hand-beaten brass beads called *khozo* are used in several ways: they can be woven together in a chain-mail effect and sewn into the fabric of *isithimba* (backskirts), *liphoto*, *jogolo* (married women's aprons) and *gabi* (pre-pubescent front skirts) or they can be used in single strings by themselves or as part of other necklaces. The *khozo* are often removed from a *liphoto* or *jogolo* before it is sold, which shows that a high value is placed on these small beads.

Udoli, Nwana and *Ntwana* / child figures

Zulu *udoli* / child figure
fabric, glass seed beads, thread
19 x 10 x 13 cm
acquired 1995 from Mordechai Brodie, Johannesburg

Tsonga *nwana* / child figure
fabric, tin, thread, glass seed beads, buttons
14,5 x 27 x 20 cm
acquired 1995 from Mordechai Brodie, Johannesburg

Northern Sotho *ntwana* / child figure
grass, fabric, glass seed beads
29 x 12,5 x 12,5 cm
acquired 1995 from Mordechai Brodie, Johannesburg

'Dolls' or 'fertility figures' are found throughout Southern Africa. They are called names such as *nwana, gimwana* and *umntwana* which mean 'child' rather than 'doll'. Some figures are made by girls at the time of their initiation (a rite which marks sexual maturity) while others are given to brides by their parents or an older woman. Ritual healers may advise barren women to construct one of these figures and to treat it as she would a child. This is thought to facilitate conception. These 'child' figures are believed to attract the sympathetic blessings of the ancestors so that they may assist a woman to find a husband, fall pregnant or bear a child.

Both the structure of the figures and the materials used are symbolically linked to the notion of procreation. The central cores of the figures are phallic in shape and are covered either with sheaths of beadwork, miniature skirts or multiple rings. These figures therefore combine male and female elements in a way that suggests sexual union.

The central cores of older figures are often made of wood, a material related to male activities. Other materials, such as beads and cloth, relate to female activities. Still others, such as gourds, grass, reeds and clay are linked to fertility and myths of genesis. These figures therefore operate, both in shape and in the material used, as talismans.

▶ Ndebele
Mporiana /
chest piece

▼ Ndebele
Mthambothi /
thambothi necklaces

▶ Ndebele
▼ *Mthambothi /*
thambothi necklaces

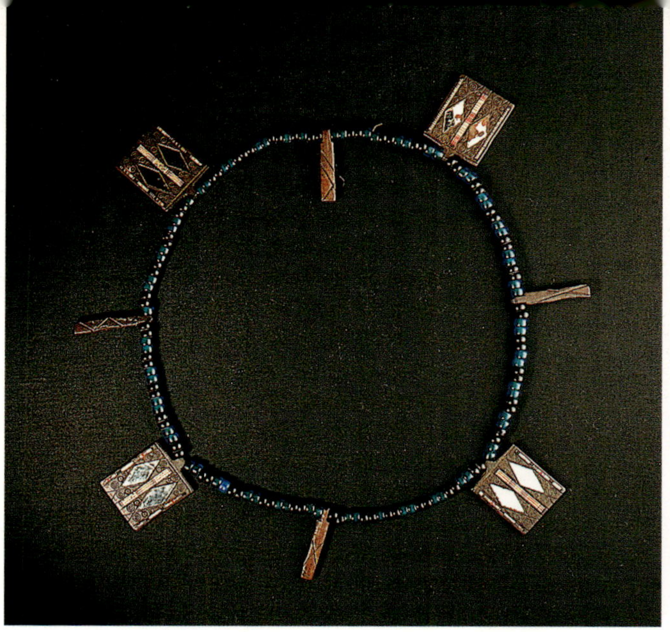

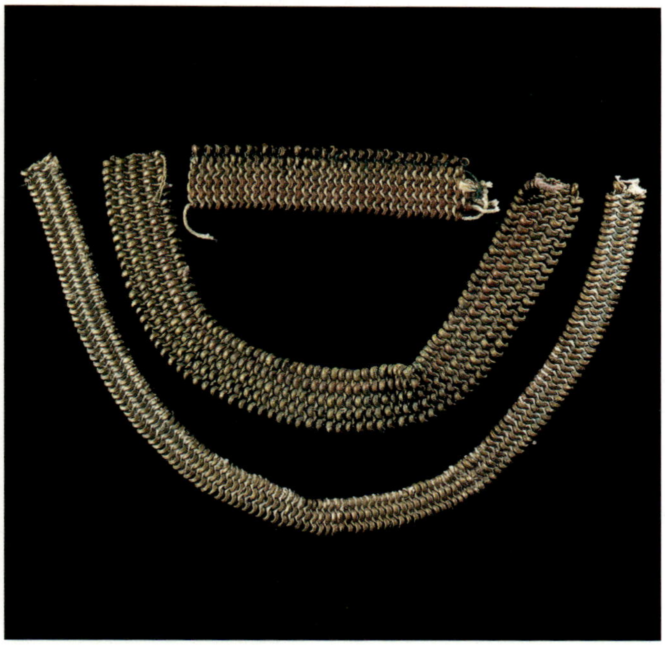

▲ Ndebele
Mthambothi /thambothi necklaces

Ndebele ▲
Khozo / brass beads

◀ Zulu
Udoli / child figure

▲ Northern Sotho
▶ *Ntwana* / child figure

▶ Tsonga
Nwana / child figure

Dzila / brass bands
brass
6,9 to 12 x 0,5 cm
acquired 1995 from Mordechai Brodie, Johannesburg

Dzila are solid brass neck, leg and arm bands, some with incised designs. These bands are worn by married Ndebele women and are given by their husbands as an indication of their wealth. Only a few women continue to wear *dzila* while many have adopted plastic, clip-on versions that can be put on or removed at any time. A woman wearing a full set of *dzila* will have 15 rings on each leg, 15 on each arm and 12 or 13 around her neck. The continual wearing of brass rings, usually with one or more large beaded grass hoops called *holwane*, causes a great deal of physical discomfort which the women themselves testify to.

Bebedwane / bead apron
glass seed beads, thread, fabric
36 x 15 cm
acquired 1995 from Mordechai Brodie, Johannesburg

The *bebedwane* is a strangely shaped piece of beadwork made by Lovedu women and for some time it was unclear how it was worn. Research has shown that it is a panel which fits over a longer triangular leather backskirt which is worn by young women undergoing initiation.

> In the old days, we all used to wear leather aprons (the older women now wear cloth skirts). When our daughters went to initiation, we made them smaller aprons similar to the ones that we wore, a triangle like the young women now wear that is made of plastic. After we got beads and learned how to make beadwork, we would decorate our clothing by placing the beads over the apron.

(Brodie, 1987: interview with Lovedu women).

Tsonga vessel
clay, paint
17 x 25.5 cm
acquired 1995 from Mordechai Brodie, Johannesburg

People who believe they have been possessed by evil or unlucky spirits will seek help from a sangoma. Different healers use different objects in the divination and exorcism process. Instruments include divining tablets of wood or bone called *hakata*, a whisk of hyena or wildebeest hair, containers with herbs and medicines and clay vessels such as these. The sangoma will mix certain substances in the pot and a large head of foam develops. Instead of sliding down the sides the flat top catches the foam creating a dramatic effect during the healing ritual. This foam is integral to the procedure.

Ehoro / milk pail
wood
31 x 35.5 cm
acquired 1995 from Mordechai Brodie, Johannesburg

Ladle
wood
29 x 11,7 x 8 cm
acquired 1995 from Mordechai Brodie, Johannesburg

The cattle herds of the Herero people of Namibia are tended by young boys but the cattle are milked every morning and evening by women and girls. The pail that a woman uses is called an *ehoro* and it is owned by her. The form is full and generous and to enhance and preserve it the wood is rubbed with a mixture of red ochre and fat in the same way as people anoint their bodies. These pails are never washed and are used until they break.

Isithebe / woven mats
plant fibre
52 x 45 cm (Bhaca)
49 x 55, 54 x 52, 88 x 92 cm (Ndebele)
22 x 26, 19.5 x 22 cm (Zulu / Shembe)
acquired 1995 from Mordechai Brodie, Johannesburg

Woven mats are ubiquitous in Southern Africa. They are made from grass or reeds and come in many sizes depending on their use. Mats in which both the warp and weft are grass are stiff and cannot be rolled, whereas sleeping and sitting mats have the warp constructed of string or other flexible material so that they can be rolled easily. These mats are stored in *amabhaxa* (storage racks) or hung on the wall.

The small tightly woven mats called *isithebe* are used by Northern and Southern Nguni under grindstones to collect spill-over of grains or as a cutting board surface on which to prepare food. Northern Nguni or Zulu mats often have intricate patterns woven into them.

Many of these show food, candle wax or other stains indicating domestic use such as the placing on them of lamps, candles, ornaments or keys. Food mats are easily washed.

Larger *isicephu* are used as sitting mats but also for wrapping aprons. *Amacansi* are used for sleeping. All these mats have multiple functions. They provide protection against dampness and insects and they define personal space which is freed for other activities when the mat is rolled up.

Xitlhekutana / skirt
fabric, glass seed beads
95 x 18 x 5 cm
acquired 1995 from Mordechai Brodie, Johannesburg

The majority of Tsonga-Shangaan people living in the Northern Province moved there from Mozambique some time between 1835 and 1900. They have developed a distinctive culture and one of their most recognisable items is the beaded skirt or *xitlhekutana* worn by adult women. The skirt is made of 18 meters of imported salempore cloth which can be bought in downtown Johannesburg. The cloth is gathered at the waist and is decorated with white beads and *xipereta* or beaded panels.

Waistpiece
hide, glass seed beads, fabric, metal studs
98 x 47 cm
acquired 1996 from Michael Graham-Stewart, London

Little is known about this beadwork. It probably dates from before 1900 and possibly comes from southern Kwazulu-Natal since it is similar to beadwork made by the Lala people.

Waistpiece
glass seed beads, thread, fabric
14,5 x 95 cm
acquired 1996 from Michael Graham-Stewart, London

This early piece of beadwork was probably worn by a young woman. A number of styles are evident in the beadwork designs and colours. The belt section design appears to be from northern Kwazulu-Natal whereas the flap designs resemble those from southern Kwazulu-Natal. The cross symbols were probably copied from Red Cross wagons. Many bead pieces display these cross-cultural features making them very difficult to provenance.

Beaded gourd
gourd, glass seed beads
20 x 8.5 cm
acquired 1996 from Michael Graham-Stewart, London

This beaded container was made to hold snuff and dates to around 1900. It probably comes from southern KwaZulu-Natal.

▲ Northern Sotho
◀ *Bebedwane* / bead apron

◀ Tsonga
Vessel

▶ Herero
Ehoro / milk pail and ladle

◀ Zulu
Isithebe / woven mat

▲ Zulu
Isithebe / woven mats

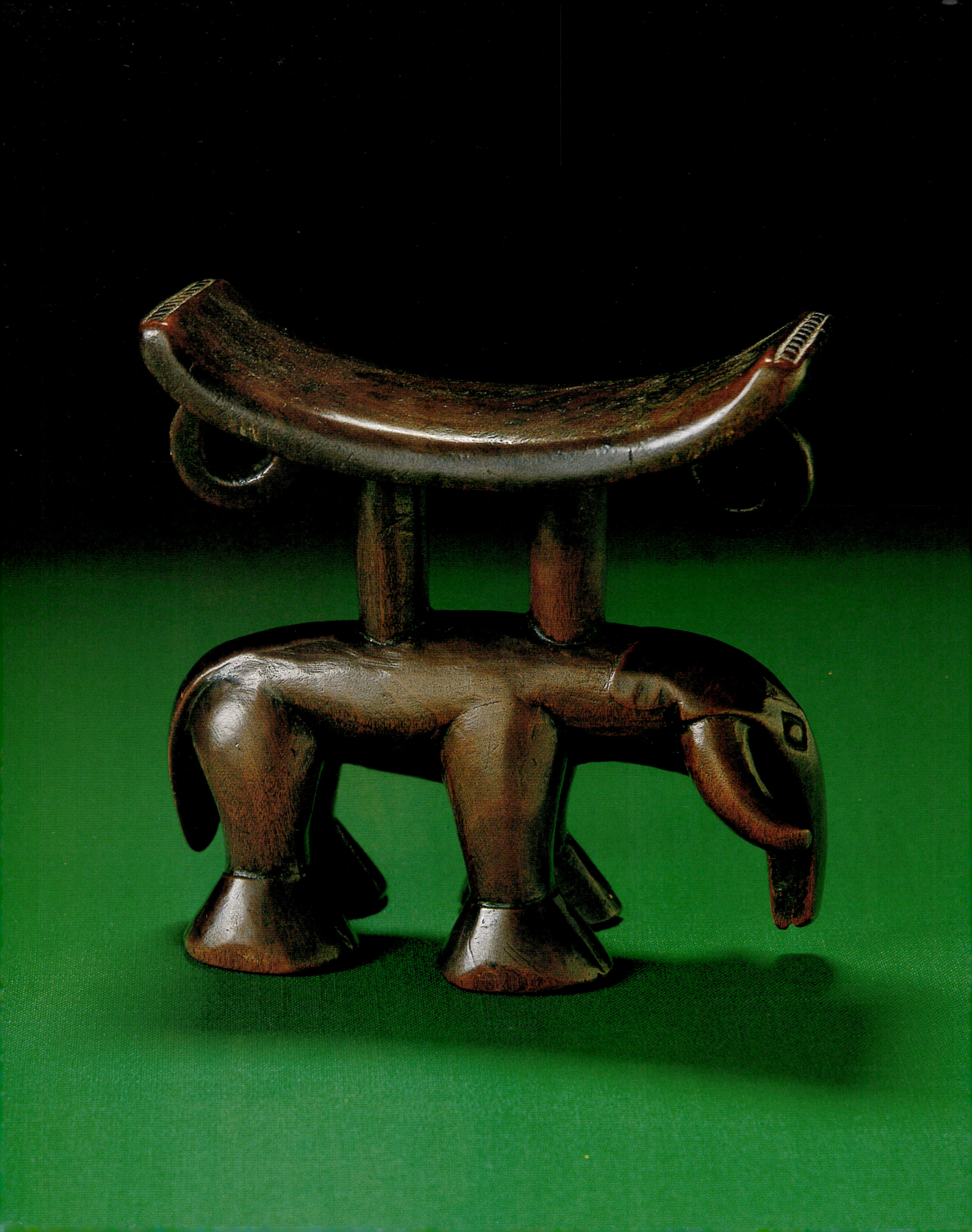

◀ Tsonga
Headrest

▲ Zulu
▲ **Headrest**

▲ Shona
▲ **Headrest**

▲ Swazi and Zulu
Headrests

Tsonga, Swazi and Zulu headrests

Tsonga headrest (elephant design)
wood
13 x 13 x 5,5 cm
acquired 1992 from Udo Horstmann, Switzerland

Tsonga headrest
wood
21,5 x 8 x 12,5 cm
acquired 1987 from the Jaques family, Johannesburg

Tsonga headrest
wood
15,5 x 18,5 x 6,5 cm
acquired 1987 from the Jaques family, Johannesburg

Tsonga headrest
wood
19 x 8,5 x 15 cm
acquired 1987 from the Jaques family, Johannesburg

Tsonga headrest
wood
20,2 x 10 x 14,5 cm
acquired 1987 from the Jaques family, Johannesburg

Tsonga headrest
wood
17 x 7,3 x 12 cm
acquired 1987 from the Jaques family, Johannesburg

Northern Nguni / Swazi headrest
wood
41,5 x 8 x 13,5 cm
acquired 1987 from the Jaques family, Johannesburg

Northern Nguni / Zulu headrest
wood
29,7 x 7,5 x 12,4 cm
acquired 1987 from the Jaques family, Johannesburg

Shona headrest
wood, metal chain
13,5 x 13 x 6,5 cm
acquired 1992 from Udo Horstmann, Switzerland

Northern Nguni / Zulu headrest
wood
14 x 35,8 x 8 cm
acquired 1992 from Udo Horstmann, Switzerland

Headrests are wooden pillows which are found in many parts of the world and have been used for thousands of years. They have been found in the tombs of ancient Egypt, in China, Japan, Polynesia and Africa. In Southern Africa, few headrests are still used for sleeping on but some have come to be valued as connections to the ancestral world. It is thought that while sleeping on the headrest you are able to enter the world of the ancestors through your dreams. Headrests also protect elaborate hairstyles by raising the head off the ground. Headrests are very personal objects and have only one owner at a time. Some are buried with the owner while others, especially those owned by a household head, are handed on to the next generation.

Headrests show a great variety of form and style. Tsonga and Shona headrests resemble each other in that they have three parts: a base, a vertical centre piece and a gently curved top section on which to rest the head. Many shapes allude to the headless human form, especially the female. The lower base of many Shona headrests is bi-lobal with sculpted genitalia between the lobes. Shona society is polygamous and these headrests were used by men who would have them placed outside the house of the particular wife with whom they wished to sleep that night. In placing his head on the headrest the man symbolically completed and re-enacted the union from which children are born – the fertility (body) of his wife combined with his ancestral line (residing in his head).

Swazi and Zulu headrests are structurally different from Tsonga and Shona ones. They are longer and do not often have a distinctive bottom section. Swazi headrests resemble cattle and have two pairs of legs with tails at either end. The legs are usually fluted and also suggest the *isidwaba* or pleated leather skirt worn by married Swazi and Zulu women. In the centre of the top cross-bar and projecting downwards is a knob which resembles an umbilicus or a penis. Similar forms are seen in Zulu headrests, although the legs and centre projection are heavier and different patterns are used.

Cattle forms are used because of their importance in Zulu and Swazi culture. They provide a link with the ancestors, they are a major source of wealth used in transactions such as the paying of *lobola* (bride price) and they are a source of meat and milk.

Pedi figures
wood, pokerwork
37 x 12 x 9,5 cm (male)
34 x 12 x 10 cm (female)
acquired 1992 from Udo Horstmann, Switzerland

Pairs of male and female figures are used as teaching aids at initiation schools in South Africa. The Pedi people belong culturally and linguistically to the larger Northern Sotho group and live mainly in the Northern Province. These figures are naturalistic and great attention has been paid to the details of dress and hair. The style of carving may have been influenced by missionary instruction and may have been created for a tourist market. This does not prevent similar figures from being used in initiation schools. One carver may produce similar types of figures for a variety of markets.

Batlokwa skirt
plant fibre, glass seed beads
20 x 80 x 11 cm
acquired 1995 from Mordechai Brodie, Johannesburg

This skirt is consistent with short skirts worn throughout Southern Africa by young maidens at the time of puberty. The bunching at the hips gives the impression of fullness, thus emphasing and enhancing her shape and status as a maiden approaching womanhood.

Tswana knife
metal, bone, hide, leather, wood
22,3 x 2,2 x 1,3 cm
acquired 1992 from Udo Horstmann, Switzerland

***Nceka* / beaded cape**
fabric, beads
134 x 114 cm
acquired 1995 from Mordechai Brodie, Johannesburg

▲ Pedi
Figures

Tswana ▲
Knife ◀

Tsonga ▲
Skirt

Tsonga ▶
Nceka / beaded cape

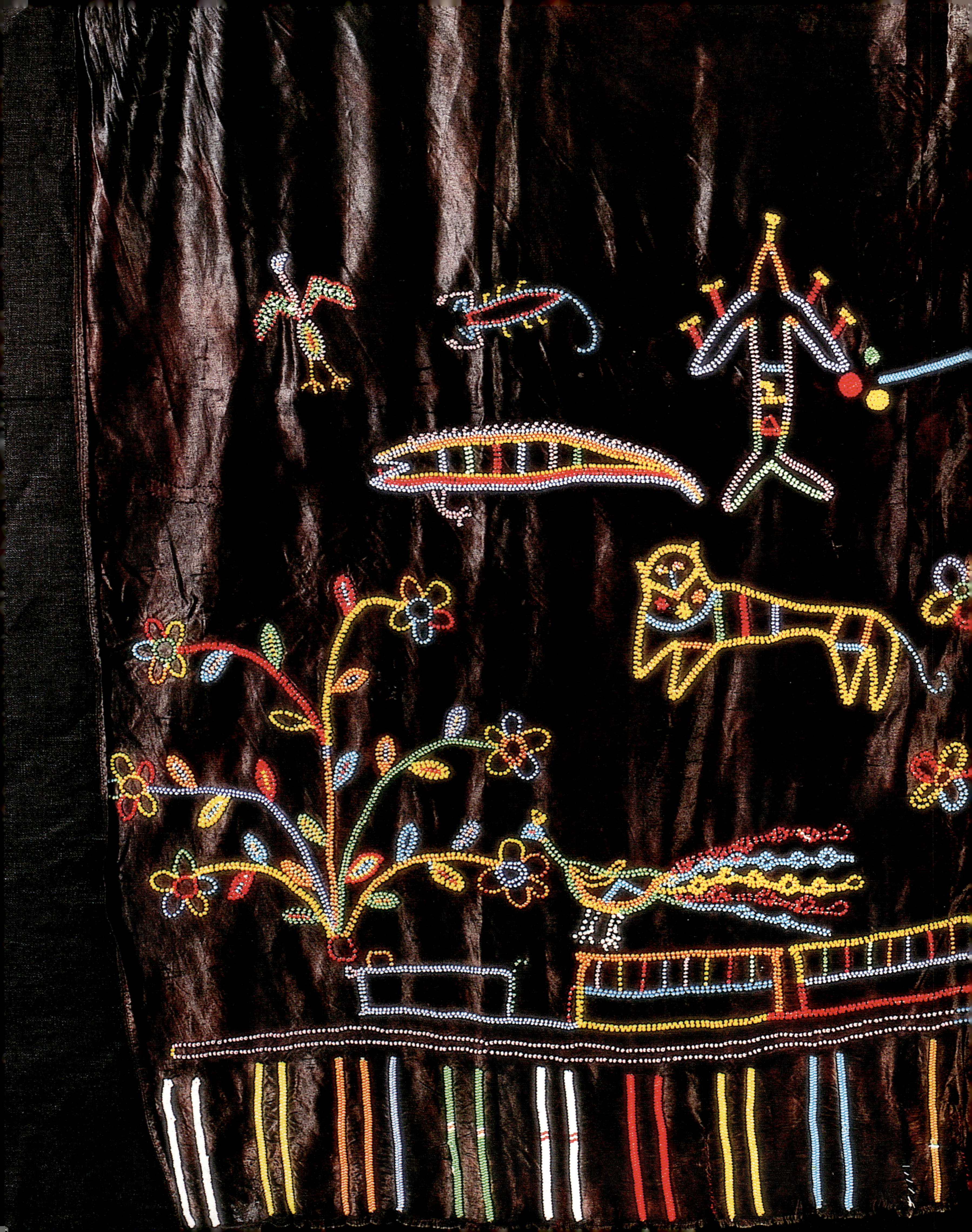

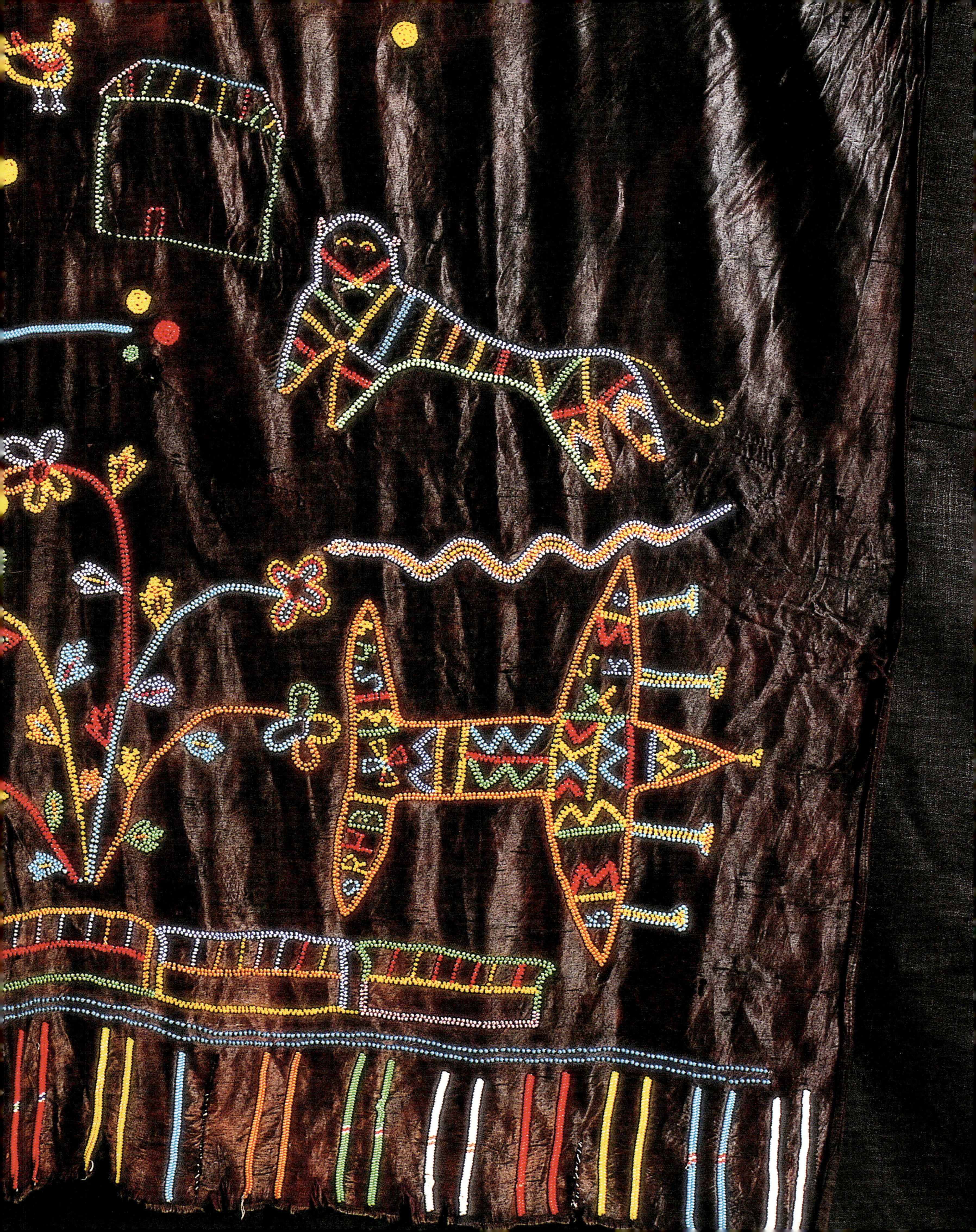

▲ Gwen John
Study for **Portrait of Miss Sarah (Biddie) Bishop** (face) 1929

The Anglo Trust and the Development of the Historic Collections

The Anglo American Johannesburg Centenary Trust has enabled the Johannesburg Art Gallery to forge radical new directions in collecting, principally in the area of traditional Southern African art. However, new directions in collecting have not been the only focus. The Trust has also contributed substantially to the historic foundation collection, reflecting its respect for 'the terms and conditions under which the Art Gallery was established and its initial collection donated' (Deed of Trust of the Anglo American Johannesburg Centenary Trust, 22 April 1986).

The Gallery was founded in 1910 as a museum of modern art, showing the best in contemporary British art-making and its artistic roots, and with the intention of expanding in certain areas such as Dutch Old Masters. The Trust has been used to enhance the foundation collection, to make it more coherent visually and historically, and thereby to make it a more effective educational tool.

The first addition to the foundation collection was a well-documented portrait by Sir William Quiller Orchardson of his daughter. This had been on loan to the Gallery from a local private owner and its acquisition not only complemented the other British portraits and Orchardson painting in the collection, but also ensured that it was retained as a national treasure within South Africa.

Subsequent historic acquisitions have been mainly in the 'British Moderns' area of the early twentieth century, enhancing the Gallery's already fine representation of artists associated with the Camden Town and Bloomsbury groups. The Trust has enabled the Gallery to purchase an early Duncan Grant portrait, a Malcolm Drummond interior, two Vanessa Bell paintings, a Spencer Gore drawing, two Gwen John water-colours, and a Gwen John portrait with related sketches. The Gore drawing is a preliminary study for a painting that has been in the Gallery's collection since the 1910s. Related studies like this and the Gwen John portrait sketches are actively sought as they enhance the educational nature of the collection with their insight into artists' working methods.

Another small but important area dating from the foundation of the Gallery is the collection of nineteenth-century Dutch Impressionists. This has been enhanced by a Bernardus Blommers scene of women mending nets.

Blommers was one of the most highly regarded and popular members of the Hague School Impressionists and the acquisition of a major painting of his has greatly enriched the Gallery's holdings. An added advantage of acquiring this work was that it came from a local collection and, like the Orchardson, it was thus secured against export.

The most recent acquisition through the Trust is a Salvador Dali modified telephone sculpture, a representative example of Surrealism in the 1930s. The Gallery had been actively seeking a Surrealist piece in order to enrich its overview of early twentieth-century art. This acquisition has considerably enhanced the Gallery's collection as an educational resource.

But perhaps the most exciting moment in the expansion of the historic collection was the discovery in 1991 of a 'lost' seventeenth-century Dutch portrait by Nicolaes Eliasz. Pickenoy. The portrait was the companion to another portrait presented to the Gallery in 1950 by Eduard Houthakker.

The tracking of the missing portrait has the air of detective fiction. The pair had been separated for over ninety years, the husband lost in one or more private collections in the USA, the wife residing for over forty years in the renowned Adolphe Schloss Collection, under the name of a different artist and without an identity. Her family coat-of-arms had been removed by an over-zealous restorer. Independent research by the Johannesburg Art Gallery and the Netherlands Institute for Art History (RKD) in The Hague established the wife's identity, the correct artist, and the fact that there was a missing husband. He finally surfaced, anonymously, at Sotheby's New York. Sotheby's contacted the Director of the RKD for identification, and a chain of events was set in motion that ended in Laurens Joosten Baack and his wife Diewer Jacobsdr. van Harencarspel being reunited.

The pursuit of objects with the help of the Trust doesn't always have this detective edge, but it is certainly always rewarding. The ability to augment the Gallery's budget with the Trust endowment means the Gallery can make purchases it could not otherwise pursue. It is immensely satisfying to curate a collection knowing the previously unattainable may now be acquired. The winners in this situation are always the museum and its general public, who ultimately own the collections we curate.

JILLIAN CARMAN
Curator: Historic Collections

▲ Nicolaes Eliasz. Pickenoy
Portrait of Laurens Joosten Baack 1629

▶ Nicolaes Eliasz. Pickenoy
Portrait of Diewer Jacobsdr. van Harencarspel 1629

Nicolaes Eliasz. Pickenoy
(1588, Amsterdam – 1650/56, Amsterdam)
Dutch School
Portrait of Laurens Joosten Baack 1629
oil on panel, 121,25 x 89,9 cm
inscribed top right: AEtatis sua.62.Ano.1629
Baack coat-of-arms top left
acquired 30 May 1991 on auction, Sotheby's New York

Pickenoy was one of the most popular portrait painters in Amsterdam during the first half of the seventeenth century. He received numerous commissions from the ruling burgher class, including large group portraits of corporations and town guards. His popularity was eclipsed in the 1640s by Bartholomeus van der Helst, a younger artist who used a more colourful palette.

This portrait and its companion piece were previously attributed to Jacob Adriaensz. Backer, Thomas de Keyser and Michiel Jansz. van Miereveld. The current attribution, based on documentary evidence, was made by Dr R.E.O. Ekkart of the Netherlands Institute for Art History (RKD) in The Hague (Ekkart, 1991).

The portraits of Laurens Joosten Baack and his wife, Diewer Jacobsdr. van Harencarspel, were formerly in the collection of H.I.A. Raedt van Oldenbarneveldt. They were separated in November 1900 at a sale in Amsterdam. Diewer Jacobsdr. van Harencarspel eventually entered the collection of the Johannesburg Art Gallery in 1950, as a gift from Eduard Houthakker. Laurens Joosten Baack was effectively lost until the portrait was brought to Sotheby's for auction in 1991.

Laurens Joosten Baack, an Amsterdam merchant, was born in 1570 in Stekenen int Lant van Waes and was buried in 1642 in the Oosterkerk, Amsterdam. He married Diewer Jacobsdr. van Harencarspel (1569-1645) in 1596. She was buried in the Oosterkerk, Amsterdam, in 1645 (Carman, 1994:54).

The portrait pair was painted in 1629 in a manner typical of that time. The wife sits on the husband's left side and is rendered subordinate not only through being placed on the supposedly weaker side, but also through adopting a more static pose. They both wear the conservative, dark clothing that was usual for wealthy Calvinist burghers of that time, with Spanish influence still lingering in the fine linen ruffs. Their wealth is not overtly expressed – and they undoubtedly were wealthy, if they could commission an artist like Pickenoy to paint their portraits. Pickenoy's exceptional abilities can be seen in the way he has captured the sitters' personalities, and in the expressive use of the hands.

Bernardus Johannes (Bernard, Bart) Blommers
(1845, The Hague – 1914, The Hague)
Dutch School
Women repairing nets late 1880s
oil on canvas, 75,5 x 125 cm
signed bottom right: Blommers
acquired 1991 from the Arts Association Namibia

Blommers was one of the most highly regarded and popular members of the Hague School of Dutch Impressionists. His popularity extended beyond Holland during his lifetime, particularly to Britain and the USA. He studied with Willem Maris at the Hague Academy and was a close friend of Jozef Israels, who had a great influence on Blommers' stylistic development. Blommers worked mainly on the coast at Scheveningen until it became too popular as a seaside resort. After about 1900 he worked in the quieter fishing village of Katwijck.

The scene is probably set on the coast at Scheveningen. Fishing boats, the sea and fisher folk provided subjects for Blommers throughout his working life. Many other artists associated with the Hague School also adopted these subjects. The colours are more sombre than those used by French Impressionists, a typical characteristic of Dutch Impressionists.

Bernardus Blommers ▲
Women repairing nets late 1880s

Sir William Quiller Orchardson R.A.
(1832, Edinburgh – 1910, London)
British School
Portrait of Hilda Orchardson 1894
oil on canvas, 128,8 x 96,1 cm
signed bottom left: W Q Orchardson – 1894
acquired 1989 from the sitter's son, Mr Philip Gray of Henley-on-Klip

The Edinburgh-born Orchardson was much admired in his day as the last great heir to the David Wilkie tradition of Scottish painting. He is renowned particularly for his genre (story-telling) paintings and portraits.

Hilda Orchardson was born in 1875 and this portrait marks the occasion of her entry into society. She was the second of Orchardson's six children. Orchardson was particularly close to Hilda, the elder of his two daughters, and used her as a model in some of his genre paintings. **The last dance**, begun in 1905 and never finished, shows Hilda and her fiancé before her permanent departure for South Africa (Hardie, 1972: introduction). The departure of his beloved daughter seems to have affected Orchardson, as his last works are generally of a melancholy nature.

Hilda married Hugh Gray, the elder brother of her best friend, in 1905. They had four sons and one daughter. Gray emigrated to South Africa in 1904 as a farm manager, after serving in the British army during the Anglo-Boer War. The couple moved to the present family farm at Henley-on-Klip in 1929. The daughter of the first curator of the Johannesburg Art Gallery, Albert Gyngell, recalls visiting the Grays' farm near Wolwehoek in the Free State, where the family lived from 1919 to 1929 (Price, 1989). Hilda died in South Africa in 1954 (Gray, 1996).

The portrait is documented in books by James Stanley Little (Little, 1897: list of chief pictures) and Cosmo Monkhouse (Monkhouse, 1901:161), and in Hilda Orchardson Gray's own biography of her father (Gray, 1930: illustration facing p 228).

Spencer Frederick Gore
(1878, Epsom – 1914, Richmond)
British School
Promenade and box at the Alhambra Theatre c 1910
lead pencil, coloured pencil and ink on paper, 35,3 x 25,4 cm
estate stamp bottom right: SFG
acquired 1995 from Davis & Langdale Company, Inc., New York

Spencer Gore is considered one of the major members of the Camden Town Group of 1911-12, which was formed in reaction against the increasingly conservative New English Art Club. He trained at the Slade School and was influenced by Walter Richard Sickert and Lucien Pissarro, who introduced him to a Neo-Impressionist Pointillist technique.

This is a study for **The Windmill Ballet**, c 1910, a painting presented to the Gallery by Sylvia Gosse in 1913. The drawing suggests the full corps de ballet scene that is shown in the painting. This is probably the act in **The Mad Pierrot Ballet**, where a windmill is part of the set (Baron & Cormack, 1980:53).

Music hall, theatrical performances and audiences constitute some of the major subjects in Gore's short career. One of his favourite venues was the Alhambra Theatre, Leicester Square, London, where he did paintings and drawings from 1906 until 1911. According to information given to Davis & Langdale by Frederick Gore, the artist's son, and Richard Shone, the art historian, the Alhambra boasted a succession of notable ballerinas from Italy, France, Denmark, Spain and Russia, as well as a variety of character, acrobatic and eccentric dancers (Davis & Langdale, 1995).

There is a sketch of a woman on the reverse of the drawing.

▶ Sir William Quiller Orchardson
Portrait of Hilda Orchardson 1894 (detail)

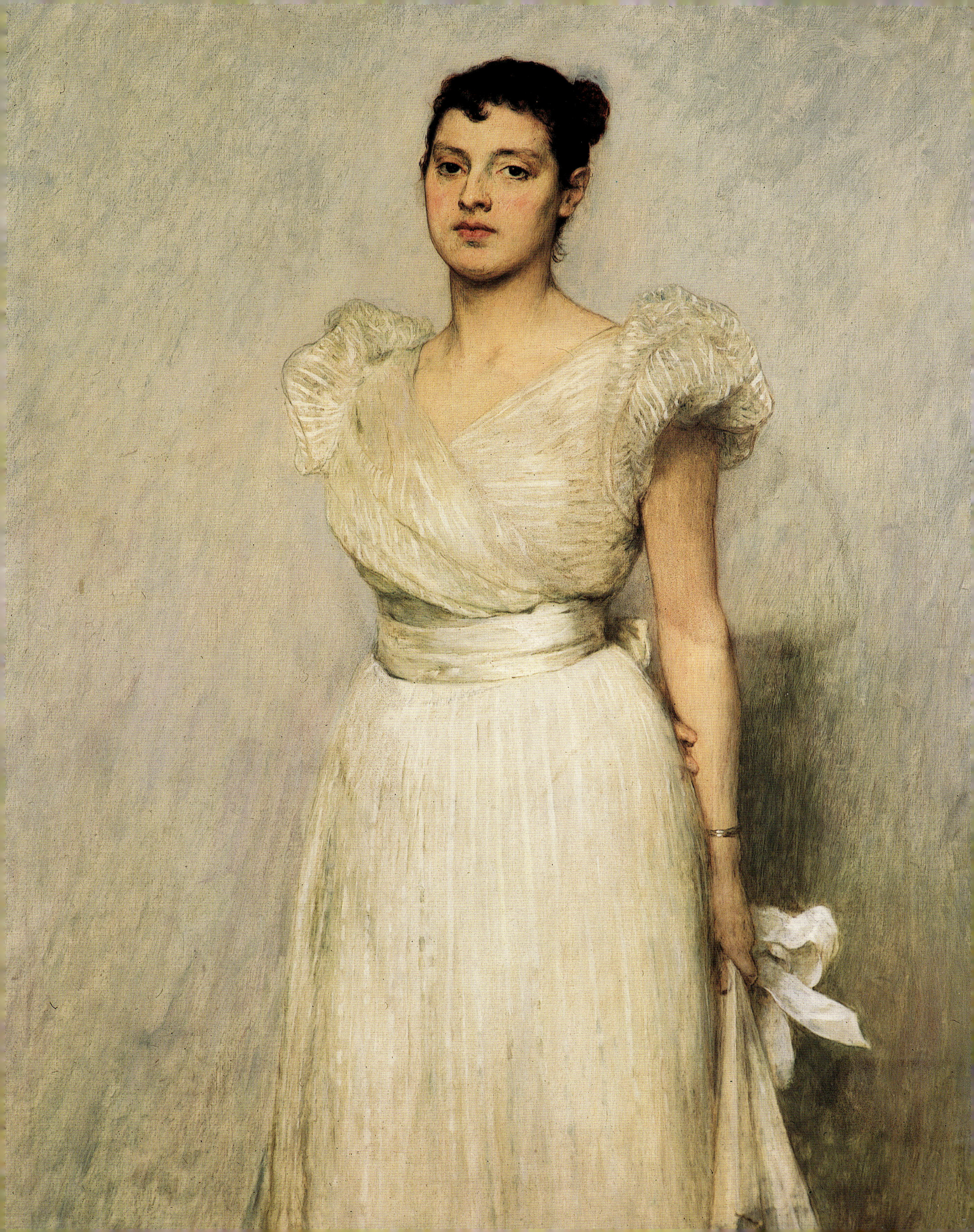

Spencer Frederick Gore ▲
Promenade and box at the Alhambra Theatre c 1910

Spencer Frederick Gore ▶
The Windmill Ballet c 1910

Malcolm Drummond (1880, Boyne Hill – 1945, Moulsford)
British School
Interior in Chelsea 1913–14
oil on canvas, 51,5 x 41 cm
signed bottom left: DRUMMOND.
acquired 1990 from the St. James's Art Group, London

Malcolm Drummond studied at the Slade School and later at the Westminster School of Art under Sickert. He was part of the Fitzroy Street Group, out of which grew the short-lived Camden Town Group in 1911 and, in 1913, the London Group. The artists associated with these groups and the Bloomsbury circle were influenced by French Post-Impressionism and represented the British avant-garde of the time. Drummond became blind towards the end of his life.

According to Drummond's son James, the interior is 16 Bramerton Street, Chelsea, where James was born in 1911. The family moved to live with James' grandfather in Maidenhead in 1914. James Drummond believes the standing woman on the left is probably his mother, Zina, and the young girl is his elder sister Elspeth, born 1907: 'That's about all, except that I think I recognise some of the furniture' (Drummond, 1990).

This type of painting is typical of the Camden Town Group – with incidental details, such as the tea-time still-life, rough dabs of colour, and a 'snap-shot' composition, as though the figures have been captured in the split second of a camera shutter.

Duncan James Corrowr Grant (1885, Rothiermurchus – 1978, Sussex)
British School
Mary St John Hutchinson 1915
oil on plywood, 68,5 x 51,3 cm
acquired 1990 from the Bloomsbury Workshop, London

Duncan Grant was part of the Bloomsbury circle with Roger Fry, Clive and Vanessa Bell and Virginia Woolf. He worked with the Omega Workshops and was a member of the Camden Town Group (1911-12).

Mary Hutchinson (née Barnes, 1889-1977), was a cousin of Duncan Grant. She married the barrister St John Hutchinson in 1910 and was Clive Bell's lover for many years. She was a valuable patron of the Omega Workshops and commissioned decorations for her house at Hammersmith and subsequently at 3 Albert Road, Regent's Park, London (Shone, 1993:169).

There are four Bloomsbury portraits of Mary St John Hutchinson, two by Vanessa Bell (one is in the Tate Gallery) and two by Duncan Grant. They were apparently all done at the same time during three days of sittings on the 5th, 9th and 11th of February 1915. The venue seems to be the Hutchinsons' London home, which was decorated by the Omega Workshops. The abstract design in the background of the portraits (especially visible in the Tate's portrait by Bell) is similar to the type of work Duncan Grant was doing at that time, for example, screens for the Omega Workshops in about 1913.

In a letter quoted by Simon Wilson (1989:131), Vanessa Bell describes how Duncan Grant 'got very desperate' during the sittings and began his painting again. The other Grant portrait is in a private collection and is reproduced by Shone in an earlier edition of **Bloomsbury Portraits** (Shone, 1976:fig.106). It is not known whether this or the Johannesburg one is the rejected first version. The Johannesburg Art Gallery also has a related charcoal drawing.

▲ Malcolm Drummond
Interior in Chelsea 1913-14

◀Duncan Grant
Study for **Mary St John Hutchinson** c 1915

Duncan Grant ▶
Mary St John Hutchinson 1915

Gwendolen Mary (Gwen) John
(1876, Haverfordwest – 1939, Dieppe)
British-French School

Portrait of Miss Bridget Sarah (Biddie) Bishop 1929
oil on canvas mounted on board, 41 x 32,3 cm
acquired 1995 from Davis & Langdale Company, Inc., New York (ex artist's estate)

Chrysanthemums in a jug late 1920s to early 1930s
gouache and watercolour on paper, 16,3 x 12,4 cm
signature stamp bottom right: Gwen John
acquired 1990 from the Bloomsbury Workshop, London (ex artist's estate)

Gwen John trained at the Slade School but soon left England for France, where she spent most of her life in the village of Meudon near Paris. She painted mainly still lifes and portraits on an intimate scale and in a style that has been described as exquisitely sensitive. Her spontaneous drawings and watercolours are as highly regarded as her oil paintings. Many historians now consider her a more interesting artist than her more famous brother, Augustus.

Portrait of Miss Bridget Sarah (Biddie) Bishop

Biddie Bishop was eighteen and studying for six months at the Sorbonne in Paris when her mother, Louise Salaman Bishop, commissioned her portrait. Louise was an old friend of Gwen John's, whom she had met while at the Slade. Gwen met Biddie, '(. . .) such a lovely little girl!' (John, 1928), soon after she arrived in Paris. The first sitting took place on 2 March 1929, in Gwen's 'logement' in the rue Terre Neuve, Meudon. Gwen selected the clothing: a navy blue coat and skirt, a dark blue cloche hat, and a blue and white Wedgwood necklace.

By late March, work was well under way: 'The portrait is getting on slowly. I am so happy with her (. . .) I think one of her beautiful qualities (. . .) is her calm' (John, 1929). There were a number of sittings, during which the artist struggled with the left arm and hand: 'As to Biddie's portrait, I cannot send it to you yet as I have not done that hand!' (John, 1930). Gwen never felt she had completed the portrait and never parted with it. It was still in the artist's studio when she died in 1939 (Langdale, 1987 and 1995).

Bridget Bishop, now Mrs Latimer, lives in London. She describes Gwen John as a quiet and retiring person who did not chat while she was working (Latimer, 1995). Her 'logement' consisted of one room 'which was bedroom, livingroom and studio with attic windows opening on to the roof through which cats were continually coming in and out. There was no running water, only a pipe and tap on the landing outside the door.' The Wedgwood necklace was still in her possession until a few years ago, when it was stolen.

Two related unfinished oils remain in the artist's estate with a number of related drawings, two of which were acquired with Anglo Trust funds for the Johannesburg Art Gallery.

Chrysanthemums in a jug

The artist painted many versions of this subject in the late 1920s. The drawn-back curtain, seen here and in the portrait of Biddie Bishop, is typical in her later works as a device that suggests the screening-off of the outside world.

Gwen John became increasingly reclusive towards the end of her life and hardly painted during the ten years before her death in 1939.

The Gallery also has a gouache painting of children in the church at Meudon, which the artist attended and where she made many sketches. This was purchased with Anglo Trust funds at the same time as **Chrysanthemums in a jug**.

Gwen John ▶
Portrait of Miss Bridget Sarah (Biddie) Bishop 1929

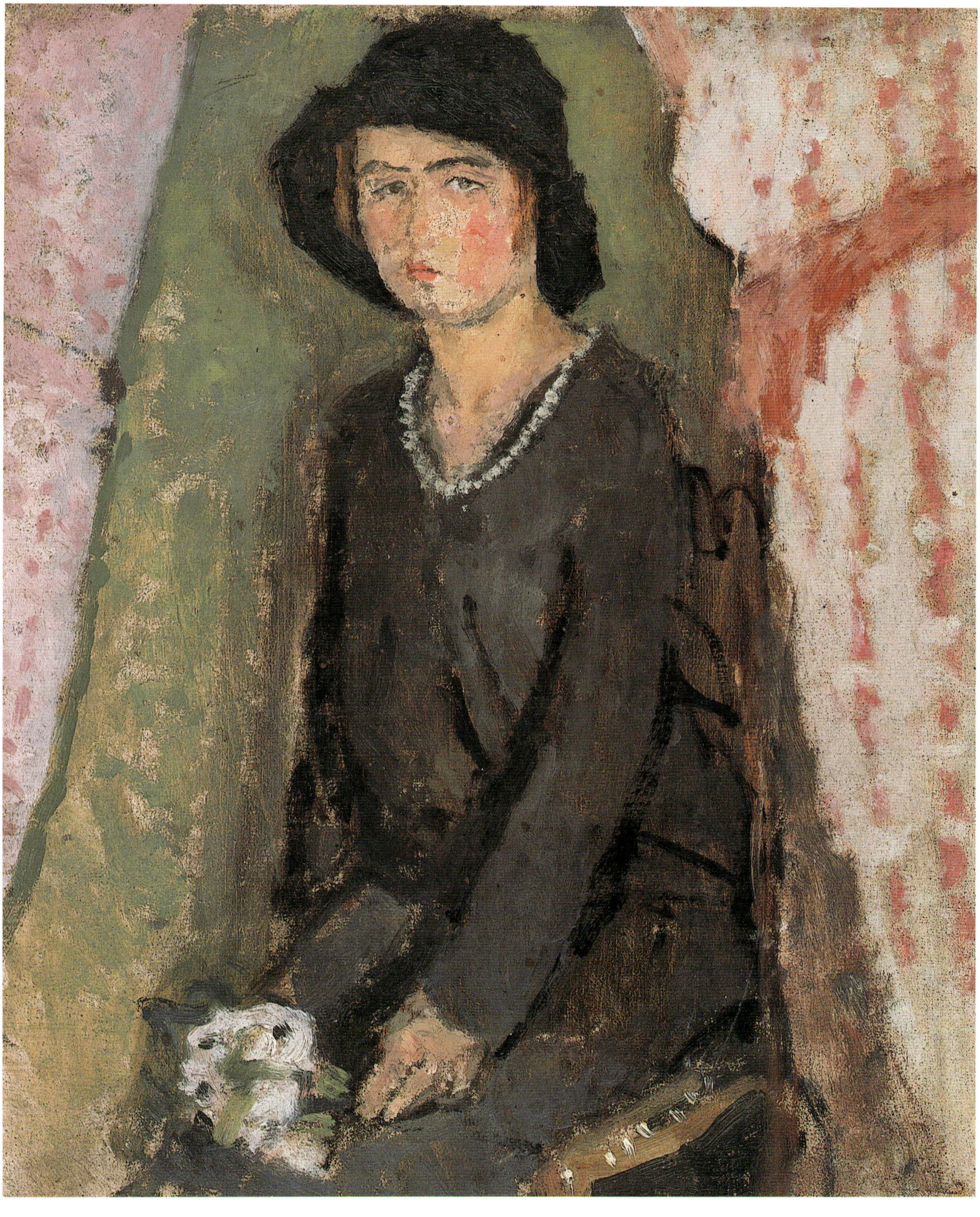

Gwen John ▲
Chrysanthemums in a jug late 1920s to early 1930s

Gwen John ▶
Children in church 1920s

Vanessa Bell (1879, London – 1961, Sussex)
British School
Mixed flowers c 1932
oil on canvas, 80,5 x 60 cm
acquired 1990 from the Bloomsbury Workshop, London
Self-portrait 1960
oil on canvas, 58,7 x 49,6 cm
signed, dated and inscribed on the reverse:
by VB. Self Portrait c 1960 belongs to D.G. [Duncan Grant]
acquired 1991 from the Bloomsbury Workshop, London

Vanessa Bell, sister of Virginia Woolf and married to Clive Bell, was a central figure in the Bloomsbury circle. She did designs for Roger Fry's Omega Workshops and collaborated on decorative schemes with Duncan Grant. She moved to a Sussex farmhouse at Charleston in 1916 and by 1939 this became a permanent home for both the Bells and Duncan Grant.

Mixed flowers

Bell painted flower pieces all her life. This painting shows a vase of flowers in her studio at Charleston – a large downstairs room that became Duncan Grant's studio too. The vase stands in front of a mirror in which the mantelpiece in the studio is reflected. According to Marion Arnold, the surrounds of the fireplace were painted by Grant in a Post-Impressionist style and the pieces of pottery in the reflection are probably Omega pottery.

> The painting is about domesticity and Bell's life voluntarily restricted to her home, and here given metaphorical expression by the use of the mirror as a framing device, enhanced by the curtain or drapery which can cover and conceal.
> (Arnold, 1990a).

Self-portrait

This is the last self-portrait painted by the artist, who is shown here in her studio at Charleston. Marion Arnold (1990b) describes how the lopsided spectacles 'frame' each eye, giving two sides to her character. The left eye (the right, as we look at the painting) is alert and intelligent, while her right eye, obscured by the spectacle frame, suggests a sense of resignation. The two sides of the canvas, in similar manner, give different aspects of the artist's life. On the left is the clutter of the studio and domesticity – jars, bowls, pictures and a sewing machine. The right side is more abstract, showing aesthetic concerns – pictorial space and a draped curtain, signifying the artifice of painting.

▲ Vanessa Bell
Self-portrait 1960

▶ Vanessa Bell
Mixed flowers c 1932 (detail)

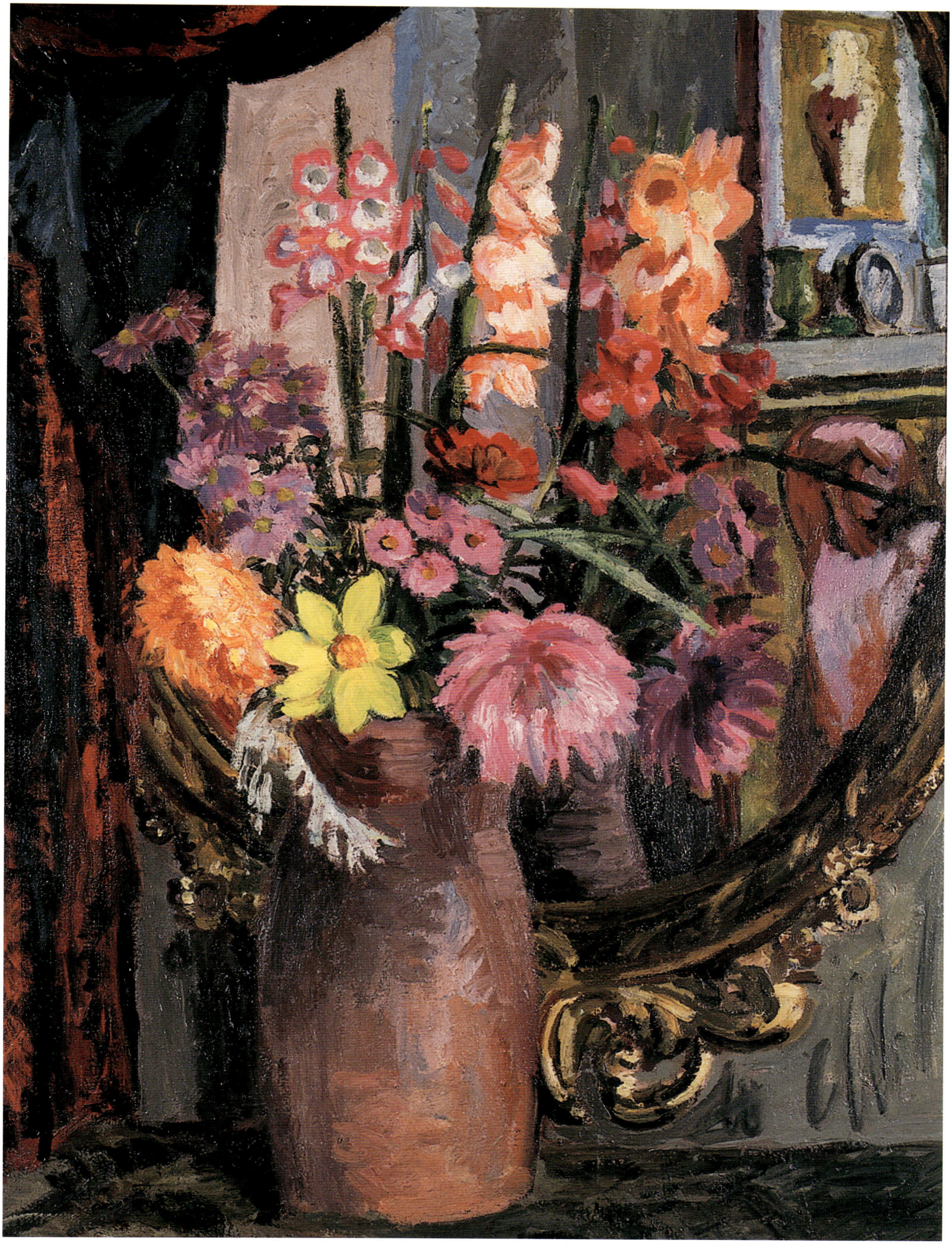

Salvador Dali
(1904, Figueras – 1989, Figueras)
Spanish School
White Aphrodisiac Telephone 1936
modified telephone (mixed media),
18 x 12,5 x 30,5 cm
acquired 1996 from the Mayor Gallery, London
(ex Edward James Foundation)

Salvador Dali was one of the most spectacular and famous members of the Surrealist movement. Arising between the First and Second World Wars, Surrealism is characterised by the belief that 'objective chance' (irrational coincidence) is central to reality. There are three main stylistic types in Surrealism: truly automatic imagery (images from the unconscious), hallucinatory or magic realism, and assemblages of unexpected and unrelated objects. For many, Dali typifies Surrealism with his hallucinatory scenes and unexpected combinations of objects. Long after the movement had disintegrated in the early 1940s, Dali continued his eccentric exhibitionism which has made him one of the household names of the twentieth century.

Edward James, an eccentric English patron of Surrealism and friend of Dali, had an arrangement with Dali in the late 1930s whereby he acquired most of Dali's best work. According to James, he and Dali were sitting on his bed at Monkton eating lobsters and throwing the shells to the side when one landed on the telephone. This gave them the idea for placing a lobster on a telephone, and James had Dali make him ten lobster telephones for use in his Wimpole Street home – four red lobsters on black bases, and six white lobsters on white bases. Today these are in collections throughout the world, including the Tate Gallery London, the National Gallery of Australia, the Boymans Museum Rotterdam and the Minneapolis Art Institute. The date of manufacture is generally considered to be 1936, although 1938 has also been suggested (Gibbs, 1995). Whichever year, they were made at the height of Surrealism.

The assemblage of two unrelated objects such as a lobster and a telephone is a typical Surrealist motif. The lobster has sexual connotations, which are emphasised in **White Aphrodisiac Telephone** by the tail (where the lobster's sexual parts are located) covering the mouthpiece of the telephone (Bernstein, 1988:19). In Dali's design for the cover of **Minotaure**, no.8, 1936, a Surrealist journal, a female figure with a bull's head has a lobster covering her sexual organs (Ades, 1978:291). One of the prostitute-like mannequins lining the entrance to the International Exhibition of Surrealism at the Galerie des Beaux-Arts, Paris, 1938, held a lobster as a telephone receiver (Sawin, 1995:4). The telephone also has a more sinister association with war. In a series of late 1930s to 1940s drawings and paintings, Dali used the telephone as a reference to Chamberlain's telephone calls to Hitler, which culminated in the Munich Agreement of September 1938 and preceded the outbreak of the Second World War (Bernstein, 1988:19).

The idea of concealing a telephone under a lobster also refers to the bourgeois practice at that time of hiding telephones behind fake books and in 'vases de nuit' (chamber pots) (Gibbs, 1995).

Salvador Dali ▶
White Aphrodisiac Telephone 1936
© DEMART PRO ARTE B.V.

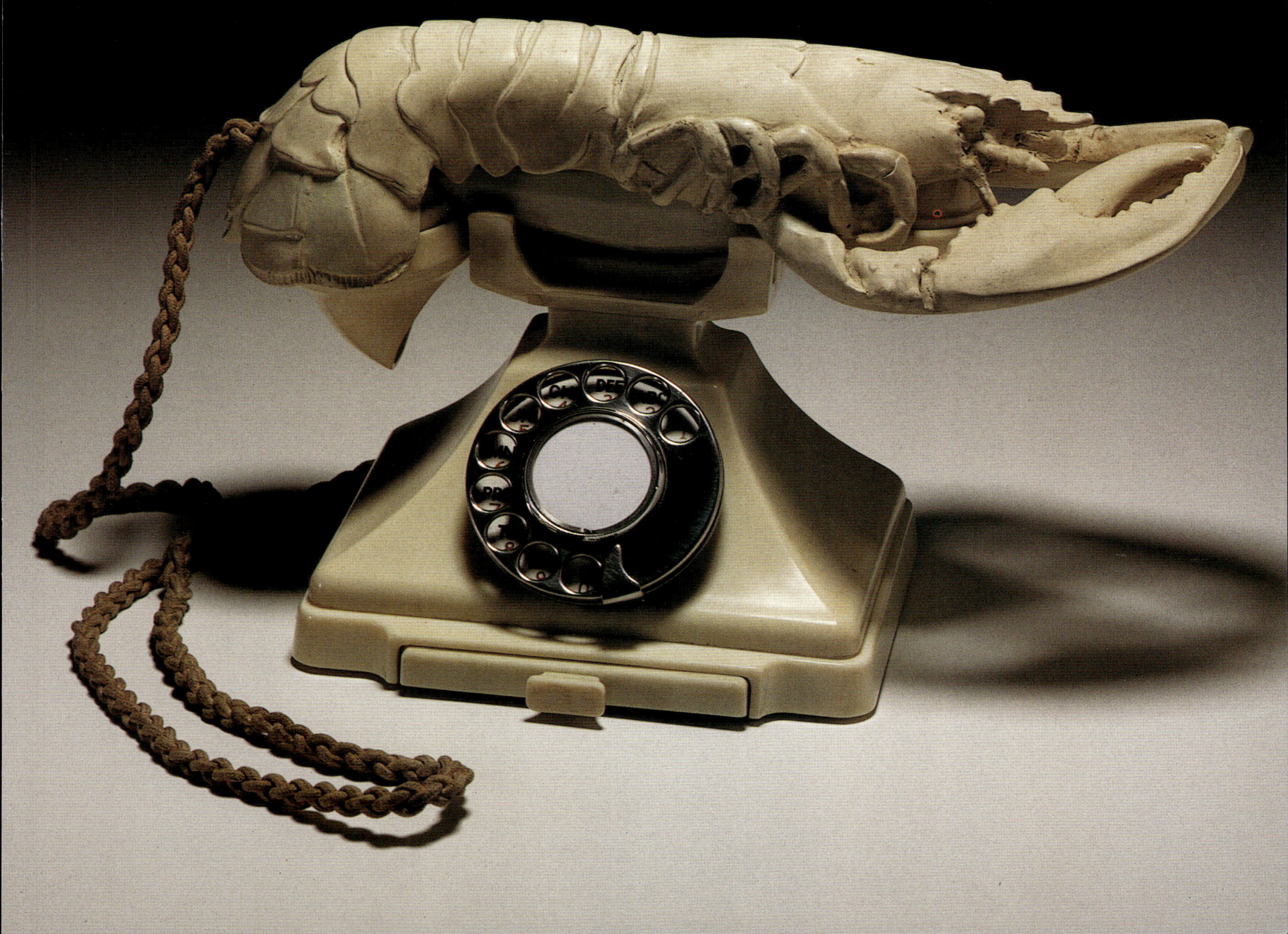
DEF

▲ Azaria Mbatha
The stranger (greeting the stranger) 1993
© Azaria Mbatha / BUS SWEDEN 1996

The Anglo Trust and the Contemporary South African and International Collections

The Johannesburg Art Gallery has an extensive collection of art by contemporary South African artists. This collection is constantly expanding, with the help of funds from the Anglo American Johannesburg Centenary Trust. The acquisition of major works of art that could not be covered by the Gallery's purchasing budget is thus made possible. Works are acquired from many different sources including commercial galleries, private owners, artists' estates and competitions as well as directly from the artists.

In some cases the works acquired with Anglo American Trust funds complement the Gallery's existing holdings of works by the same artists. **Rose as Olympia** 1966 by Stanley Pinker (b 1924, Windhoek) was acquired in 1989. This significant early painting augments the paintings and drawings by this important Cape-based artist already in the collection.

Three sculptures were selected from entries to the 1990 Johannesburg Art Gallery Sculpture Competition. All practising artists in South Africa were invited to submit maquettes, with the intention of finding suitable sculptures for the west sculpture garden. One maquette, **Coming home** 1990 by Gavin Younge (b 1947, Bulawayo) was acquired and two sculptures were commissioned: **African icon** 1992 by Peter Schütz (b 1942, Germany) and **For those taken darkly** 1990-1993 by Andries Botha (b 1952, Durban). These major bronze sculptures are important additions to the Gallery's holdings of sculptures and prints by these artists.

Measure of the city 1962 by Selby Mvusi (1929, Pietermaritzburg-1967, Kenya) was acquired in 1995 and was subsequently joined by the donation of another work by this influential teacher, academic, poet and artist.

Works by local artists living outside of South Africa who have established important international reputations are also collected. **The voice of the turtle** 1989 by Ansel Krut (b 1959, Cape Town) was acquired in 1993. Krut is currently based in England. **Sleeptime** 1992 by Doris Bloom (b 1954, Vereeniging) was acquired in 1994 and **Self portrait as a mannequin** 1992 by Pamela Melliar (b 1961, Bulawayo) was acquired in 1996. Bloom lives in Denmark and Melliar in England. These are the only works by these artists in the Gallery's collection. **L'Ancêtre** 1969-1971 and **Untitled** c1958-1966 by Ernest Mancoba (b 1904, Johannesburg) were acquired in 1994. The acquisitions in 1996 of **La double unité** 1950, **Untitled** 1959 and **Drawing V2** 1993 complete the Gallery's holdings by Mancoba, who lives in France.

The stranger (greeting the stranger) 1993, **Passion Jesus** (Mapumulo) 1962, **The ark** 1993 and **The vision for a new world** 1993 by Azaria Mbatha (b 1941, Mabeka) were acquired in 1996. These are valuable additions to the Gallery's collection of prints by this significant artist now based in Sweden.

The Anglo American Johannesburg Centenary Trust Fund also enables the Gallery to continue expanding its collection of international contemporary works. This collection provides vital access to international art trends especially for educational purposes. Collecting international works has become increasingly difficult, however, due to factors such as financial constraints, South Africa's unfavourable exchange rate and import surcharges. In 1987 a decision was taken in response to these considerations to concentrate on building up the contemporary international print collection. Because prints are multiple works of art produced in limited editions, they are more affordable than one-off works such as paintings and sculptures.

As with the South African contemporary collection, some prints acquired through the Anglo American Johannesburg Centenary Trust complement works by the same artists already in the collection. **Crak!** 1964 by Roy Lichtenstein (b 1923, United States of America) which was acquired in 1990, and **Venice, evening** 1995 by Howard Hodgkin (b 1932, Britain) which was acquired in 1996 greatly enhance the Gallery's existing holdings of prints by these eminent artists.

Painter 1983 by Philip Guston (1913, Canada -1980, United States of America), acquired in 1990, **Kai** 1992 by Lucian Freud (b 1922, Germany) and **Alex** 1992 by Chuck Close (b 1940, United States of America) both acquired in 1994, are the only works by these world-renowned artists in the collection.

Flowers fight 1989 by Sandro Chia (b 1946, Italy) was acquired in 1990 and is an exception to the emphasis stated in the Gallery's collecting policy on the printmaking medium in that it is a multiple rather than a print (1994:16). Multiples are three-dimensional objects produced in limited numbers and are therefore, like prints, more affordable than unique artworks. **Boîte** 1968 by Marcel Duchamp (1887, France-1968, France) is also a multiple and was acquired in 1996.

Another exception is **Reclining lady** 1988 by Fernando Botero (b 1932, Columbia). This drawing was acquired in 1990 and is a significant addition to the Gallery's collection of drawings.

In South Africa, the field of contemporary art continues to be an exciting, dynamic area. As the international spotlight focuses on South African art, more opportunities for local artists to exhibit and study abroad are likely to result in growing numbers achieving international recognition. The ongoing collection of international contemporary art provides an important context within which to situate contemporary South African art. The Johannesburg Art Gallery also acknowledges an African context as critically important, and it is this area of the contemporary collection that needs active augmentation.

JULIA CHARLTON
Curator: Contemporary Collections

Gavin Younge ▶
Coming home 1990

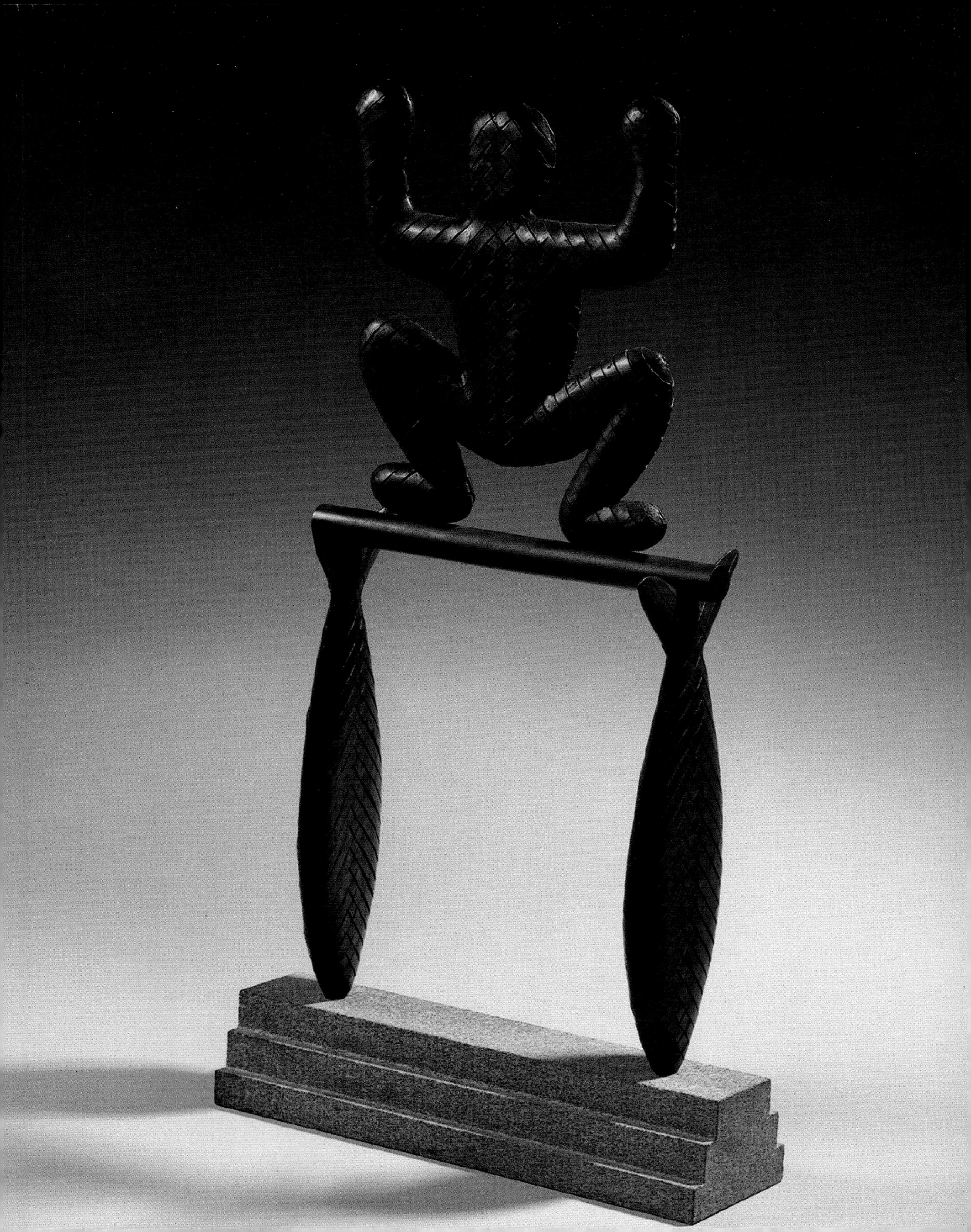

Gavin Younge (b 1947, Bulawayo)
Coming home 1990
bronze, granite, 98 x 52,1 x 15,5 cm
(including base)
acquired 1991 from the artist, Cape Town

Gavin Younge moved to South Africa in 1955. He obtained a Masters degree in Fine Art from the Michaelis School of Fine Art, University of Cape Town, where he has taught since 1975.

Younge was a finalist in the 1990 Johannesburg Art Gallery Sculpture Competition. He submitted **Coming home** as a second stage maquette which the Gallery acquired as a finished sculpture. Younge's representational work combines his overt political and strong formal concerns. In a statement submitted with his maquette, the artist writes:

> **Coming home** represents in allegorical form the reunification of our society. On a personal level, this refers to family and friends, on a broader level, it refers to nationhood and cultural identity. Inverse juxtapositions abound. Fish out of water kiss the ground of their birth as they dive headlong back into it. They cast off engagement from the drama they support; woven fish traps which have become their negation. The image of a figure crouches in an ambiguous but celebratory posture. Invoking the heroism of a dance unto death, the figure slides into shadows full of hope. **Coming home** is a celebration of a return to an imagined wholeness, that home we all hope we will have.
>
> (Younge, 1990)

Ernest Mancoba (b 1904, Johannesburg)
L'Ancêtre c 1968-71
oil on canvas, 92,3 x 60,3 cm (framed)
acquired 1994 from the artist, Paris

Ernest Mancoba was known as a sculptor when he left South Africa in 1938. He has lived in Europe since then and has achieved international recognition as a painter associated with the CoBrA movement (1948-1951). The name of this influential group is an acronym derived from the capital cities of the founder members' native countries; Copenhagen, Brussels, Amsterdam. Mancoba did not adopt the CoBrA style which is characterised by spontaneity, intense colour and expressive brushmarks. He was, however, attracted by its open-minded attitude and spirit of inclusion.

In **L'Ancêtre** Mancoba pays tribute to his African heritage and particularly his mother, whose storytelling kept the family history alive (Miles, 1994:32). **L'Ancêtre** was inspired by Kota reliquary figures from Gabon. These guardian figures are made from wood and metal and are mounted on containers that hold a family's ancestral remains. The muted colour and dispersed, directional brushstrokes are characteristic of Mancoba's paintings.

Ansel Krut (b 1959, Cape Town)
The voice of the turtle 1989
oil on linen, 130 x 200 cm
acquired 1993 from Gillian Jason Gallery, London

Ansel Krut is a South African-born artist who has achieved international recognition and is currently living in England. He has a Masters degree in Painting from the Royal College of Art, London and is represented in a number of important British collections.

This figurative artist regards art history as vitally important for contemporary art practice (Gale, 1996). His paintings draw on narrative and history painting traditions and call to mind artists such as Francisco Goya (1746-1828) and Edouard Manet (1832-1883). Krut assembles figures into mysterious theatrical masquerades that convey a sense of something important but undisclosed happening. As the artist writes in a statement supplied at the time of the acquisition:

▲ Ansel Krut
The voice of the turtle 1989

◀ Ernest Mancoba
L'Ancêtre c 1968-71

This is a painting about absurdity. In a barren landscape a figure without his trousers confronts a delegation of sombre faced men. The delegation is grave and dressed in dark clothing. These men have about them an air of invested authority, that of government, perhaps, or the law, or religion. The single figure they confront has lost his trousers, but kept his hat, his shoes, and his dignity. He is not alone, because the figures we glimpse in the background are obviously kin to him in some way, but he is an individual set apart from the undifferentiated mass of the delegation. He is on trial though, as in Kafka's **Trial** the charges are obscure. (It is enough that there are charges, their exact nature is not important.) The trouserless protagonist of this painting is caught in a situation where he is not only vulnerable and exposed but where the rules of normality have been suspended. The landscape is ruined, the sky raw, the single tree dead.

The title is from the **Song of Songs** by Solomon. The poem has become illogical in translation – there are turtles where there should be turtle doves. Turtles are mute. What could be more absurd, and more terrifying, than the erased voices of the mute, the blank moments where voices ought to be.

'Rise up my true love and come away
Spring is here
and the voice of the turtle is heard in the land'

(Krut, 1993)

▶ Pamela Melliar
Self portrait as a mannequin 1992

Pamela Melliar (b 1961, Bulawayo)
Self portrait as a mannequin 1992
clay, paint, artificial hair, granite
137 x 55 x 59 cm (including base)
acquired 1995 from the artist, London

Pamela Melliar obtained a Fine Art degree from the University of the Witwatersrand, Johannesburg and a Masters degree in Art History and Theory from the University of Essex. She was awarded a British Council Scholarship and has achieved substantial international recognition.

Melliar's powerful figurative sculptures explore the gulf between the idealised body images promoted in the media and the physical reality of what people look like. In the catalogue that accompanied her 1995 exhibition **Objects for dangerous feelings** Melliar states:

> **Self portrait as a mannequin** attempts the inversion of a one way relationship between the pornographic object and viewer through the dislocation between the figure's body and not-pretty face. While the body bends in an attitude of unconditional invitation, the figure's gaze acts as a mirror, reflecting the viewers' own potential nakedness and liability. The Self Portrait is a piece about eroticism, but the erotic element has more to do with the uneasiness provoked by the difficulty of achieving a safe position in relation to the piece . . . I have purposely set out to raise an emotional response from the viewer, although I have not intended to repulse or alienate. I have tried to make each figure as beautiful as possible in spite of its ugliness. The resulting tension is something the viewer may simply find disturbing. Beyond this, however, exists the possibility for empathy and reconciliation. But it is an unstable position, reflecting the precariousness of human relationships.

(Melliar, 1995:12)

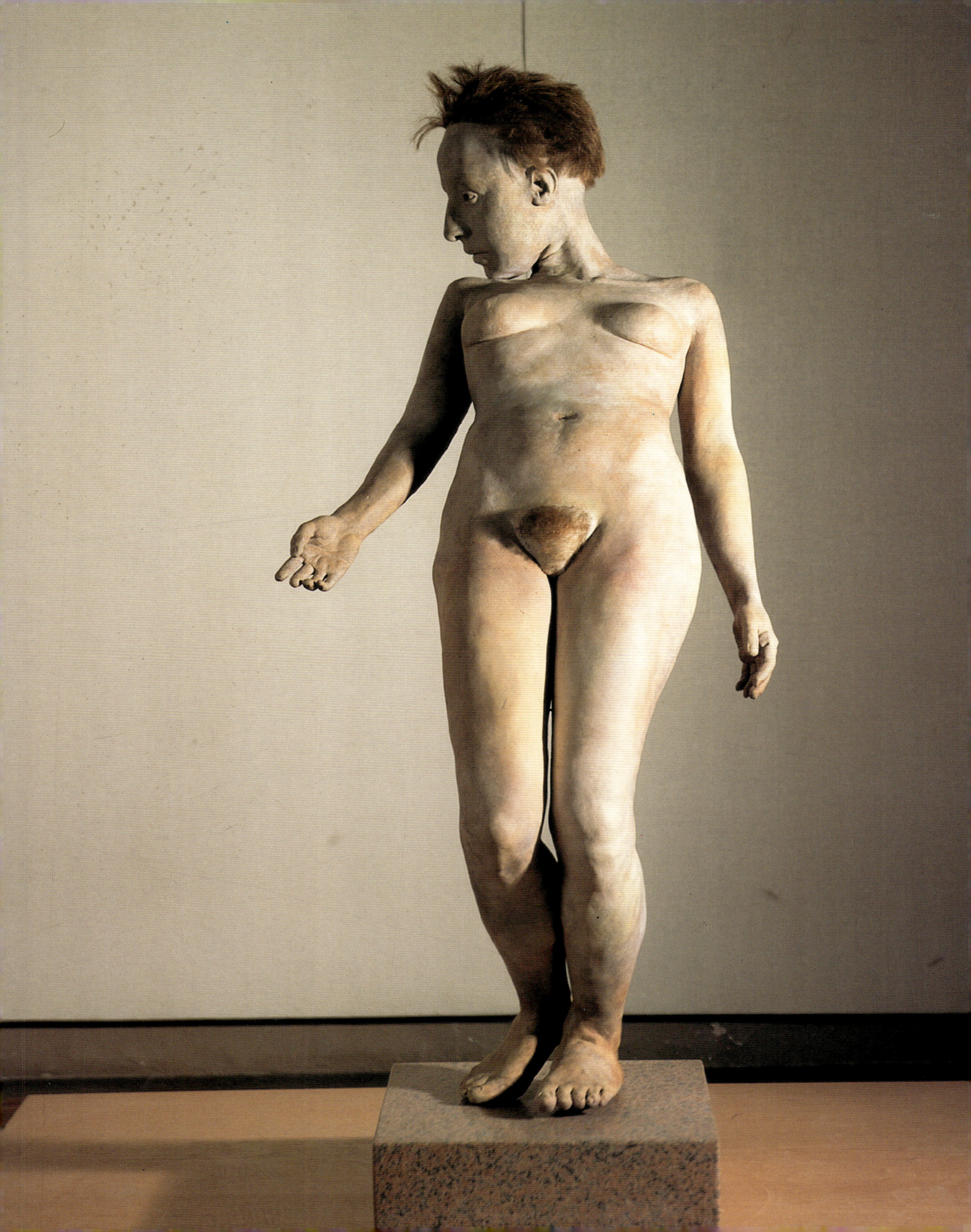

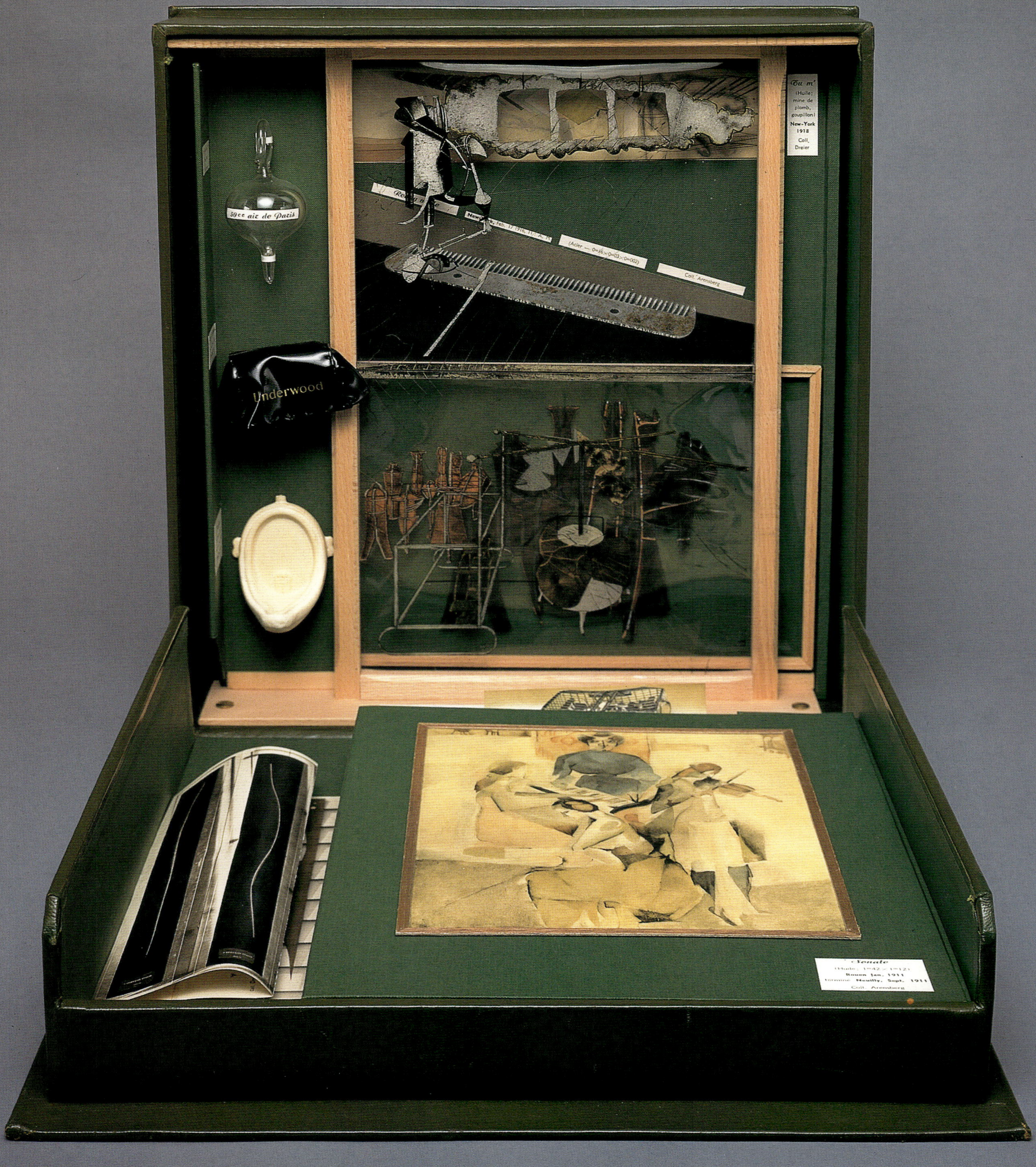
Tu m'
(Huile:
mine de
plomb,
goupillon)
New-York
1918
Coll.
Dreier
air de Paris
Underwood
Sonate
Rouen Jan. 1911
Neuilly, Sept. 1911

Azaria Mbatha (b 1941, Mabeka)
The stranger (greeting the stranger)
1993
linocut, 205 x 292 cm (framed)
acquired 1996 from Gallery on Tyrone, Johannesburg

Azaria Mbatha was one of the first students in the early 1960s at the Evangelical Lutheran Church Art and Craft Centre at Rorke's Drift, Natal. Since 1970 he has lived in Sweden and achieved international recognition. Mbatha is represented in many European and American museums including the Museum of Modern Art in New York.

The stranger (greeting the stranger) was commissioned by the Department of Development Education in Germany and Switzerland. Each year an international artist is invited to interpret the theme of the *Lenten Veil*, the practice of covering crucifixes with cloths during Lent. Mbatha was selected to represent Africa and **The stranger (greeting the stranger)** is the 1994 *Misereor Lenten Veil*. Reputedly the largest linocut ever made, this complex image depicts six narratives. Biblical references are combined with contemporary social comment: the stories of Emmaus, Abraham and Moses emerge alongside depictions of violence, refugees, hospitality and displacement (Mbatha, 1995).

Roy Lichtenstein (b 1923, United States of America)
Crak! 1964
offset colour lithograph, 48,9 x 70,3 cm
acquired 1990 from Waddington Graphics, London

Roy Lichtenstein is one of the best known American Pop artists. The Pop Art movement is characterised by a focus on subjects taken from popular culture and a rejection of traditional 'high art' imagery, materials and methods.

Commercial printmaking techniques were enthusiastically adopted by many Pop artists. Lichtenstein appropriated both his imagery and style from comic books, magnifying the black outlines and dots typical of cheap printing to call attention to his printed source: reproduction itself is the subject of his work (Howard, 1995:82). The apparent detachment of his style, however, is often combined with dramatic and emotionally charged subjects (Wilson, 1990:232). **Crak!** is a cartoon image of war in which a patriotic fighter in a beret fires her rifle. The passion and heroism portrayed is lightened by Lichtenstein's distinctive irony.

Marcel Duchamp (1887, France – 1968, France)
Boîte 1968
mixed media multiple, 41,5 x 38,5 x 9,9 cm
acquired 1996 from Entwistle, London

Marcel Duchamp, along with Pablo Picasso, is regarded as one of the most influential artists of the twentieth century. He is associated with movements such as Dada (1915-1923) and Surrealism (1924-1945) but his work remains highly individual and resists classification. Duchamp consistently challenged traditional ideas about art and art objects. He is credited with inventions such as ready-made sculptures (existing objects given new identities as artworks), kinetic sculptures (sculptures that contain moving parts) and conceptual art (art in which the idea is more important than the object).

Boîte is a multiple, that is a three-dimensional object produced in a limited number. The first box was issued in 1941 and, over a period of 27 years, 300 were made in seven series. This box is part of *Series G* which was assembled after Duchamp's death by Jacqueline Monnier, his stepdaughter. She also assembled three previous series of boxes under Duchamp's direction, starting in 1960. **Boîte** contains 80 miniature replicas of Duchamp's most important works and is an independent work of art as well as an inventory (Naumann, 1996:26). This portable museum encapsulates the ideas in Duchamp's work as a whole and explores ideas of appropriation, originality and reproduction which continue to influence contemporary artists.

◀ Marcel Duchamp
Boîte 1968 (detail)
© Estate Marcel Duchamp - DACS (England), DALRO (South Africa)

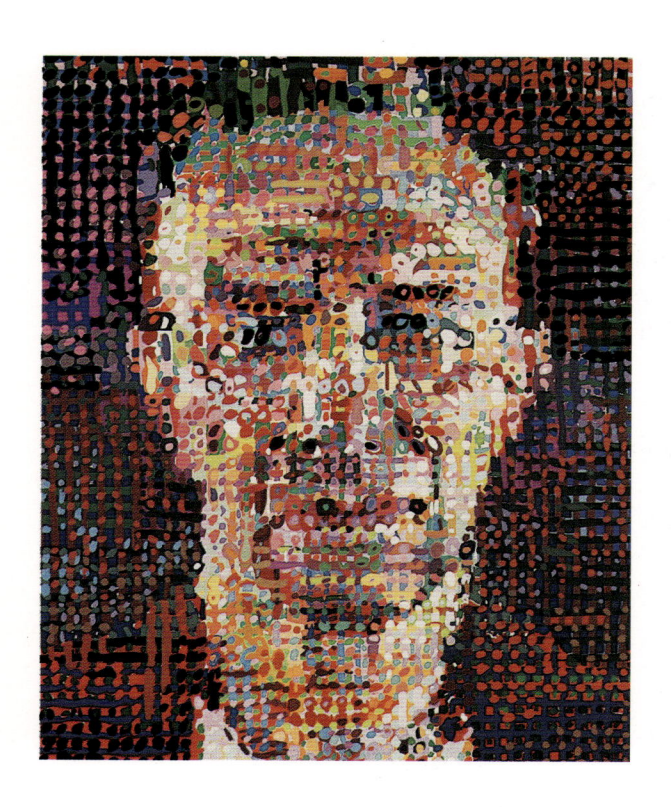

▲ Chuck Close
Alex 1992

▲ Philip Guston
▶ **Painter** printed 1983

▶ Roy Lichtenstein
Crak! 1964
© Roy Lichtenstein

Philip Guston
(1913, Canada - 1980, United States of America)
Painter printed 1983
lithograph, 81,3 x 108 cm
acquired 1990 from Waddington Graphics, London

Philip Guston first became known as a principal member of the New York School of Abstract Expressionism. His work, however, grew progressively more figurative, and the late works are characterised by a vocabulary of schematic images in surrealistic combinations. The mood of these works is a sombre blend of the everyday and the macabre.

Painter was published posthumously by Gemini print publishers in Los Angeles. It presents an alternative, ironic version of 'the artist at his canvas'. Diagrammatic renderings of a heavily bandaged face, smouldering cigarette and profiled eye are drawn in Guston's distinctive blunt black line. Subversive forms of popular culture, for example underground comics and toilet-door graffiti, are alluded to by his crude markmaking and his focus on details such as the fingernails and the tacks down the side of the canvas.

Chuck Close (b 1940, United States of America)
Alex 1992
colour wood-block print, 72,5 x 59 cm (irregular)
acquired 1994 from the Goodman Gallery, Johannesburg

Chuck Close is a world-renowned American artist who pioneered Photo-Realism in the 1960s with his large frontal portraits painted from photographs. He does not accept commissions; his subjects are snapshots of himself and his friends. Close's emphasis is on process and the creative act itself. He has developed strategies to distance himself from the subject and the viewer. These include the imposition of a visible grid on top of the faces so that the image can be assembled from a distance but disintegrates into segments when seen close up.

Close enjoys the technical challenges posed by printmaking (Stein, 1994:96). **Alex** is a portrait of the artist Alex Katz (b 1927, United States of America). The print was made with Keiji Shinohara, a Japanese master wood-block printer. 165 colours and 86 blocks were used in this fascinating collaboration between contemporary art and traditional Japanese printmaking techniques.

Howard Hodgkin (b 1932, London)
Venice, evening 1995
hand-painted etching and aquatint with carborundum, 160 x 196,5 cm
acquired 1996 from the Goodman Gallery, Johannesburg

Howard Hodgkin is a world-renowned British artist who has received many prestigious awards including a knighthood in 1992. His work is highly individual and resists attempts to classify it according to any style or movement. Brilliant colour and characteristic bars and dots make up his distinctive language of abstract form.

Hodgkin's paintings are distillations of his responses to specific experiences. **Venice, evening** is one of four prints in the **Venetian views** series which depicts a Venice scene at four different times of day. Hodgkin has experimented with a wide variety of printmaking media. Five plates were used in **Venice, evening** which is made up of 16 sheets of paper. Intense blue was painted onto the paper before and after printing, altering the intensity of the printed marks (Hartley, 1995). This process, which took over a year to complete, blurs the usual boundaries between painting and printmaking.

▲ Howard Hodgkin
Venice, evening 1995

References

Ades, D. 1978. **Dada and Surrealism Reviewed.** London: Arts Council of Great Britain.

Arnold, M. 1990a. Letter in the Johannesburg Art Gallery archives. 15 Jan.

Arnold, M. 1990b. Letter in the Johannesburg Art Gallery archives. 18 Oct.

Baron, W. & Cormack, M. 1980. **The Camden Town Group.** New Haven: Yale Center for British Art.

Bernstein, J. 1988. **Surrealism in the Tate Gallery Collection.** Catalogue of the Tate Gallery, Liverpool. Liverpool: Tate Gallery.

Brodie, M. 1985. Interview with Ndebele Women in the Johannesburg Art Gallery archives.

Brodie, M. 1986. Interview in the Johannesburg Art Gallery archives.

Brodie, M. 1987. Interview with Lovedu Women in the Johannesburg Art Gallery archives.

Carman, J. 1994: **Seventeenth-century Dutch and Flemish paintings in South Africa. A checklist of paintings in public collections.** Johannesburg: Johannesburg Art Gallery.

Davis & Langdale. 1995. Catalogue entry provided with invoice # 4533. Johannesburg Art Gallery archives 10 July.

Deed of Trust of the Anglo American Johannesburg Centenary Trust. 1986.

Drummond, J. 1990. Letter in the Johannesburg Art Gallery archives. 9 Aug.

Ekkart, R.E.O. 1991. Copy of letter from Ekkart to Sotheby's in the Johannesburg Art Gallery archives. 23 April.

Gale, I. 1996. Ansel Krut. In **Ansel Krut.** Exhibition Catalogue. London: Jason & Rhodes.

Gibbs, C. (Trustee of the Edward James Foundation) 1995. Notes in the Johannesburg Art Gallery archives. 19 Nov.

Gray, H. Orchardson. 1930. **The life of Sir William Quiller Orchardson.** London: Hutchinson.

Hardie, W.R. 1972. **Sir William Quiller Orchardson** R.A. Edinburgh: Scottish Arts Council.

Hartley, C. 1995. Venetian Views. In **Howard Hodgkin: Venetian Views** 1995. Exhibition Catalogue. London: Alan Cristea Gallery.

Hocking, A. 1973. **Oppenheimer and Son.** Johannesburg: McGraw-Hill.

Howard, J. 1995. Reflections on 'The Prints of Roy Lichtenstein'. The Print Collector's Newsletter, vol.XXVl(3):82-86, Jul.-Aug.

Johannesburg 1910. **Johannesburg municipal gallery of modern art. Illustrated catalogue.** Prefatory notice by Hugh Lane, biographical notes compiled by G. Campbell Ross. Johannesburg: Argus.

Johannesburg Art Gallery 1984/1985. Annual report.

Johannesburg Art Gallery 1994. Collecting policy.

John, G. 1928. Letter from Gwen John to Louise Salaman Bishop. 11 Oct. Quoted in Langdale, 1987:177.

John, G. 1929. Letter from Gwen John to Louise Salaman Bishop. 22 Mar. Quoted in Langdale, 1987:178.

John, G. 1930. Letter from Gwen John to Louise Salaman Bishop. 18 Nov. Quoted in Langdale 1987:178.

Krut, A. 1993. Letter in the Johannesburg Art Gallery archives. 8 Jul.

Langdale, C. 1987. **Gwen John.** With a catalogue raisonné of the paintings and a selection of the drawings. New Haven and London: Yale University Press.

Langdale, C. 1995. Material relating to Gwen John in the Johannesburg Art Gallery archives.

Latimer, B. 1995. Letter in the Johannesburg Art Gallery archives. 2 Sept.

Little, J.S. 1897. **The life and work of William Q. Orchardson**, R.A. The Art Annual, Christmas 1897. London: The Art Journal Office.

Mbatha, A. 1995. **1994 Misereor Lenten Veil.** Johannesburg: Gallery on Tyrone.

Melliar, P. 1995. **Objects for Dangerous Feelings.** Exhibition Catalogue. Bradford: City of Bradford Metropolitan Council.

Miles, E. 1994. **Ernest Mancoba: a Resource Book.** Johannesburg: Johannesburg Art Gallery.

Monkhouse, C. 1901. **British Contemporary Artists.** London: William Heinemann.

Naumann, F.M. 1996. 'The valise and box in a valise: a brief history of Marcel Duchamp's portable museum' in **The portable museums of Marcel Duchamp: de ou par Marcel Duchamp du Rrose Selavy.** Exhibition catalogue. London: Entwistle.

O' Connor, T.P. 1915. Late Sir Hugh Lane. A Lusitania victim. **A.Y.**, 21 May 1915. Press cutting in Tate Gallery archives.

Price, E. 1989. Communication in the Johannesburg Art Gallery archives. 20 July.

Sawin, M. 1995. **Surrealism in Exile and the Beginning of the New York School.** Cambridge: Massachusetts Institute of Technology.

Shone, R. 1976. **Bloomsbury Portraits: Vanessa Bell, Duncan Grant and their Circle.** First ed. London: Phaidon.

Shone, R. 1993. **Bloomsbury Portraits: Vanessa Bell, Duncan Grant and their Circle.** Paperback ed. London: Phaidon.

Stein, D. 1994. Chuck Close: 'it's always nice to have resistance'. **ARTnews**, Vol.93(1):95–96.

Wilson, S. 1989. **Tate Gallery: An Illustrated Companion.** London: Tate Gallery.

Younge, G. 1990. **Coming home.** Statement included in submission for the Johannesburg Art Gallery West Sculpture Garden Competition. Johannesburg Art Gallery archives.

Bibliography

Carman, J. 1988. Acquisition policy of the Johannesburg Art Gallery with regard to the South African Collection, 1909–1987. **South African Journal of Cultural and Art History,** vol.2(3):203–213.

Dudok van Heel, S.A.C. 1985. De Schilder Nicolaes Eliasz. Pickenoy (1588–1650/56) en Zijn Familie, **Liber Amicorum: Jhr. Mr. C.C. van Valkenburg's**-Gravenhage: Centraal Bureau voor Genealogie.

Fraser, M. (ed.) 1986. **Some Reminiscences: Lionel Phillips**. Johannesburg: Ad Donker.

Gutsche, T. 1966. **No Ordinary Woman: the Life and Times of Florence Phillips**. Cape Town: Howard Timmins.

Grossert, J.W. 1978. **Zulu Crafts**. Pietermaritzburg: Schuter and Schooter.

Hammond-Tooke, D. and Nettleton, A. 1989. **Ten Years of Collecting (1979-1989).** Exhibition Catalogue. Johannesburg: University of the Witwatersrand Galleries.

Johannesburg Art Gallery (ed.) 1991. **Art and Ambiguity: Perspectives on the Brenthurst Collection of Southern African Art.** Johannesburg: Johannesburg Art Gallery.

Johannesburg Art Gallery (ed.) 1992. **The Horstmann Collection of Southern African Art.** Johannesburg: Johannesburg Art Gallery.

Kanfer, S. 1993. **The Last Empire: De Beers, Diamonds, and the World**. New York: Farrar Straus Giroux.

McTeague, M. 1984. The Johannesburg Art Gallery: Lutyens, Lane and Lady Phillips. **The International Journal of Museum Management and Curatorship,** vol.3(2):139–152.

Miles, E. 1994. **Lifeline out of Africa: the art of Ernest Mancoba**. Cape Town: Human & Rousseau.

Naylor, C. (ed.) 1989. **Contemporary artists: 3rd edition**. Chicago and London: St James Press.

Nettleton, A. 1990. **Dream Machines: Southern African Headrests**. South African Journal of Art and Architectural History 1(4): p 147-154.

Osborne H. (ed.) 1987. **The Oxford Companion to Twentieth-Century Art**. Oxford: Oxford University Press.

Powell, I. 1995. **Ndebele: A People and their Art**. Cape Town: Struik..

Rankin, E. 1994. **Images of metal: post-war sculptures and assemblages in South Africa.** Johannesburg: Witwatersrand University Press, University of the Witwatersrand Art Galleries.

Till, C. 1986. The role of the Art Gallery and Museum in the community. **Optima,** vol.34(3), Sept.